Frances Elliot

Diary of an Idle Woman in Italy

Frances Elliot

Diary of an Idle Woman in Italy

ISBN/EAN: 9783742854520

Manufactured in Europe, USA, Canada, Australia, Japa

Cover: Foto ©Thomas Meinert / pixelio.de

Manufactured and distributed by brebook publishing software
(www.brebook.com)

Frances Elliot

Diary of an Idle Woman in Italy

COLLECTION

OF

BRITISH AUTHORS

TAUCHNITZ EDITION.

VOL. 1224.

DIARY OF AN IDLE WOMAN IN ITALY
BY
FRANCES ELLIOT.

IN TWO VOLUMES.

VOL. II.

DIARY

OF AN

IDLE WOMAN IN ITALY.

BY

FRANCES ELLIOT,

AUTHOR OF "PICTURES OF OLD ROME."

COPYRIGHT EDITION.

IN TWO VOLUMES.

VOL. II.

LEIPZIG

BERNHARD TAUCHNITZ

1872.

CONTENTS

OF VOLUME II.

———

6   CONTENTS OF VOLUME II.

AN IDLE WOMAN IN ITALY.

CHAPTER I.

The Artists' Festa.

ONE day, and another day, had been talked of for the artists' festa, annually celebrated at Rome, unless wars, or rumours of wars, or bloody red republicanism scare the old walls of the Cæsars from their propriety.

A certain Monday was fixed, and we set forth, a merry circle, chiefly of American friends, determined, like the charity children sent down by the railway for an excursion in the country, "to make a day of it." Eight o'clock saw us emerging from the Porta Salara, with its *entourage* of beautiful villas, each enshrouded in woods of laurel, box, and ilex, traversed by long vista-walks of clipped yew and cypress heavy in unbroken shade, with terraces bordered by statues, and balustrades leading down long flights of majestic

steps to the sparkling fountains below—abodes
such as no land but Italy can boast. Just now
the gardens are full of roses, flowering everywhere
in luxuriant masses, specially the white and yellow
Banksian roses, which fling themselves over the
high walls, and festoon the very trees with
wondrous-clustered blossoms. Honeysuckles, tulips,
and bright ranunculuses caught our passing sight
in the gay parterres. Especially, too, did I admire the groves of Judas-trees, real mountains of
purple blossoms, without a single green leaf to
break the gorgeous colour. They are generally
planted near the marble basins of the fountains,
in advance of the deeper woods which serve as
an admirable background. How much have those
to learn who never beheld the glorious burst of
spring in this luxuriant land! that idyllic season
realising all the glowing descriptions of the poets.
The process of renewed and opening life, occupy-
ing long months in the cold North, mysterious
Nature here accomplishes in a few days. The
land, radiant with new life, puts on its vernal
mantle of freshest green, its jewels of brightest
flowers; even the sullen rocks and frowning ruins
are embroidered with garlands of snowy May, and
flowering grasses stream in the soft breeze. The
turf becomes a perfect garden—cyclamens, ane-

mones, crocuses, violets, poppies, and hyacinths growing in such profusion, that the sweet blossoms are wantonly trodden under foot. The woods too, those primæval fortresses of ancient trees, are painted with every tint and shade of green, and vocal with innumerable nightingales, whose soft songs invite one to wander under the chequered shade, beside cool bubbling brooks and splashing fountains, all overarched by the heavens, serenely, beautifully blue.

At length we bade adieu to the zone of villas clasping like an enchanted circlet the grim city walls, and entered the Campagna—a sea of emerald green. In the direction of the Porta Salara it is beautifully varied by accidents of wood and dale, high waving headlands, and broad moory valleys, through which old Tiber flows majestically down from the fat lands of Tuscany. After descending a rocky ravine, we drove along a spacious level plateau, through which the river sweeps in many windings, bordered by hills—a region of wild craggy dells and far-stretching fells and hills, some black, rocky, and dreary, others clothed with low woods and stunted shrubs, crowned here and there with a ruined tower, or an old tomb standing out sharply against the sky. We were reminded of the object of our drive by meeting now and then a masker gaily caparisoned, on horseback; a poursuivant, all crimson and quarterings; or Stenterello, the Southern brother of "Punch," dressed in white; or a Chinaman in flowered drapery of chintz—most incongruous apparitions in that prairie wilderness. Behind, between the parting hills, uprose the great dome of St. Peter's, sole evidence of the neighbouring city. After an hour's space we crossed the Ponte Salara, a fine old Roman bridge, built by Belisarius, and drew up at the Torre, close by an ancient tomb, surmounted by a mediæval tower, in whose foundations an "Osteria" shelters itself— ruin upon ruin, all desolate and decayed. Here a dense crowd of maskers were awaiting the arrival of the president of the sports, grouped at the base of the old tomb. Such a medley: *diamine! par impossibile!* Austrian generals mounted on donkeys, wearing great stars and orders of painted pasteboard, fighting imaginary duels with wooden swords bearing the motto, "*Non amazzo;*" hunters with guns, yards long, quite suitable to Glumdalclitch in a sporting mood; Mercury, fat and rosy, in a tin helmet, fringed chlamys, boots, and pantaloons; a negro; Hercules with his club, in Turkish trousers and worsted slippers; Don Quixote, with a real brass barber's basin on his

head, riding a mule; and Ganymede, painted all
over with bacchanalian devices, such as decorate
wayside public-houses in this land of the vine;
his shoulder-knots the bottoms of rush wine-flasks,
and ivy and grapes painted all over his clothes—
a walking "*Spaccio di Vino.*" He had no sine-
cure, by the way, Ganymede, pouring out the
wine to the thirsty throng, all that livelong day.
There were soldiers and gendarmes magnificent
on donkeys which kicked, and now and then
rolled in the road; and Venetians, in red velvet
and pointed hats (recalling the dark gondolas,
shooting through the bridges, and love, and in-
trigue, and mystery, and cloudless skies, and
snowy churches, and tinkling guitars in dear
Venice); and a male Pomona, embroidered all
over with amber satin apples and green leaves;
and the great sea-serpent on horseback, much
encumbered by the wind continually catching his
tail; also a priest of Jupiter with a patched eye;
Chaucer in a red mantle, with gold bells, and a
close blue hood with a tail, and pointed shoes,
wearing spectacles too; and a Bedouin Arab, who
drove out in a small gig made of basket-work,
and invested himself with appropriate drapery of
black and white in a quite off-handed manner,
holding the horses' reins in his mouth, after which

he offered us coffee out of a large pot; Medea
driving about in an easy *calèche* with two old women—getting in every one's way, and causing
those gallant souls, the donkeys, to kick; and
Paul Pry, with an eye-glass as big as his head,
together with an unfortunate gentleman in black,
of the melancholy time of our own first Charles;
others in ruff and doublet, and hat and feathers,
of the Spanish or Raleigh school. Many characters, however, were quite indescribable, fluttering all over with oceans of variegated ribbon,
others nearly buried in flowers, and some
crowned with ivy and with bay—the only wreath,
possibly, they may ever win, so let them enjoy it
pro tempore, poor souls! Harlequins and Shylocks
—quite correct from the traditions of the Ghetto;
a schoolboy with his satchel and tight-fitting
"whites;" a Greek with red cap and mantle looking die-away and romantic; a mediæval page,
pretty enough to please "a fair lady's eye;" the
Postillon de Longjumeau in pink and white, a
dapper little fellow bestriding a huge horse, and
a *vetturino* in long boots and a laced coat.

But I have done: how can I describe one-half,
or give the faintest idea of that motley *charivari*,
merry, noisy, many-coloured? The troops of
donkeys, some laden with splendid mediæval

heroes in a red stocking, perhaps two; horses
bearing gentlemen in mufti—steady married men,
"who would not condescend, could not think," &c.,
of such tomfoolery; the waving banners, the trumpets, the braying of the innumerable donkeys
(which evidently felt themselves specially ill-used
and victimised on this occasion, and with reason),
the laughter, the cursing of the cabmen (to speak
nationally) who had come out from Rome, and
were indignant at any interference with their
wretched cattle (one little man in particular got
so violent, and gave utterance to such a volley of
Italian oaths, I thought he would have had a fit;
indeed, he was only stopped by the Austrian
general belabouring him with his wooden sword),
the Babel of languages, English, American, German, French, Italian, each louder than the other,
but the Teutonic guttural decidedly predominat-
ing, as did the artists of that nation.   In the
midst of this universal hubbub, all eyes were suddenly directed to the bridge, where appeared a
Red Indian crowned with waving ostrich's feathers
clad in skins, embroidered and edged with rich
fringes, wearing a necklace of coral and big shells,
his face painted and streaked with black, and
crimson, and brown, mounted on a big horse
covered with leopard-skins.   His quiver and ar-

rows were slung at his back, and with a rifle in
his hand he galloped forward in a wild, reckless
way, looking altogether quite terrific. Never did
I behold such a happy masquerade. He was received with shouts of applause as he dashed over
the bridge, and he had not been on the ground
five minutes before three different artists implored
him to sit to them for his portrait. Next went
forth the cry that the president was coming, and
the Germans cried "Platz!" and the Italians
"Largo!" and the English "Make way," and a
passage was cleared through the crowd for a huge
triumphal car slowly passing over the bridge,
wreathed and enveloped with laurel, and olive,
and bay, containing a knight of portly and noble
bearing, clad in cloth of gold, and wearing a
helmet. This was the president, a very Bacchus-
god, whose broad, smiling countenance told of
merry nights spent with boon companions over
the rich wine, more than of days of study. His
helmet was garlanded with vine and ivy leaves,
and he looked the very condensation of the frolic,
good-humour, cosmopolite jest and merriment of
the festa. Yes, he was well chosen, that president: and there was a large and genial soul under
that massive, manly form, that looked out from
his pleasant blue eyes, dancing with glee as he

bowed and waved his helmet, while the thrilling shouts arose of "Hoch lebe der Präsident!" "Evviva!" "Hurrah!" joined to the firing of mimic cannons, the inarticulate shouts and cries of many dialects, the braying of the donkeys, and the imprecations with which Medea and the two old ladies driving in the easy *calèche* were loaded for eternally getting in everybody's way.

Then the president, sitting royally on his car, distributed medals to all the artists present, quite appropriate to the occasion, being half *bajocchi* (the very smallest copper coin) strung with blue ribbon; these were fastened in the button-hole, and worn along with the tin drinking-cups every-body—the married dignitaries, as also the melancholy Charles I. characters—slung over his shoulders. The ambassadors were then presented; the Chinaman and his attendant, bearing an umbrella over him of brown holland, covered with dragons and monsters in coloured paper; and the Turkish minister, and the Grand Llama, and the Red Indian. Speeches were made — the deep, manly voice of the president often audible—and then songs were sung, and after that all the cavalry, the gendarmes and distinguished military authorities on donkeys, and lastly, the foot, were marshalled on the grass of the surrounding Campagna. One unfortunate little donkey, bearing a heavy cavalier, out of sheer desperation, positively lay down and rolled at the gate, overcome by the prospect of its manifold misfortunes. But it wouldn't do; he was dragged up and forced to join in the muster, and then the procession was formed—the president in his pagan car, drawn by great white oxen with scarlet housings, leading the way, followed by the banners and the horse and donkeymen, Medea in the easy *calèche*, now fairly under way, the Bedouin in his basket-gig, and lastly, a cart loaded with barrels of wine, wreathed with laurel and bay, which poor Ganymede will have to distribute, running about on those fat legs all day. Then the carriages fall in, and we all go driving farther out into the green wilderness so desolate and fair, along the river's bank, whose murmuring waters are rarely drowned by such strange sounds of holiday. The solitary road along which we pass is overshadowed by the past; the merry present finds there no sympathy: hills rise around, and beyond, on the opposite bank of the river, wooded heights stretch far away into infinite space, sweeping over the plain towards the far distant, just visible Monte Soracte; and near by are rocks of a sunburnt, ruddy tint, protruding through the grass in the fissures of the

hills, giving a wild, characteristic look to an otherwise monotonous scene.   We reach an opening
opposite the river, flowing away with full majestic
stream to the left; a broad valley, broken by a
stream, cleaving asunder the low, rounded heights,
and winding away through red-looking rocks, with
nothing but a few ragged shrubs and tufted grass
and brambles clinging to their sides.   It is a sad
and lonely place, like some old battle-ground
heavy with the curses of the slain.   There are
deep grottoes, too, in the rocks, and on one side
a precipitous mound of black stones and broken
earth, difficult of access.   On the summit of this
mound the artists' banner is planted, and flutters
gaily in the wind; for it is a fresh and breezy
day, divided between delicious wafts of sea breezes
and a southern sun.   Under the rocky mount a
tent is erected for the dinner, beneath whose
shade the ponderous wine-barrels are piled, followed by Ganymede ever in close attendance;
and the president now, descending from the
triumphal car, assembles his motley court on the
hillside.   The whole valley is peopled with incongruous groups of maskers scattered here and
there; hundreds of spectators bivouac among the
fissures, and crevices, and chasms of the rocks,
and recline on *improvviso* divans on the fresh

An Idle Woman in Italy. II.   2

grass, forming a vast human amphitheatre, to witness the games below on the level ground. Loud
laughter and sounds of mirth soon arouse the
echoes of the hills, especially when Ganymede
emerges from the tent, and rushes frantically about,
bearing the wine-cup.

The games are announced. First came a
donkey-race—those unhappy victims of the artists'
rejoicing—with piteous brayings, being forced to
carry large men, who urged them across a stream,
which they positively refused. Few would go at
all, being utterly regardless of the feelings of the
mailed knights, and ambassadors, and nobles of
high degree they bore, and the whole race ended
in a grand *mêlée* and confusion. A thing very
like a gibbet was then erected for riding at the
ring, the riders being arranged on one side all
bearing lances, with which, dashing forward, they
were to carry off the ring from the hook. Chaucer,
with his cap and bells, got a fall, Pomona rolled
on the grass in company, and the Chinese ambassador, whose long plaits of tow he evidently
considered a masterpiece, tumbled on the top of
both; the Red Indian carrying off the ring amid
shouts of laughter echoing from hill to hill. This
game was repeated many times with various suc-
cess; then the wine-bowl passed round, and the

deep bass voice of the president was heard en-
couraging the sports; while the indignant donkeys
brayed louder and louder, waking the whole Campagna with fresh fun and frolic. At last, when
the sun had become intolerably hot, and the Bedouin had long settled himself down in the shade
to drink coffee out of his large pot, the dinner
was announced, and the president and his court,
and the masquerade company generally, adjourned
to the tent, where for the space of two hours
they were lost to mortal ken under the shadows
of the great wine-casks. Knots formed, too,
among the spectators for eating and drinking, but
there was no shade, not even a bush, to temper
the sun's rays on the burning Campagna that
mocked one with its fresh mantle of emerald
green. I ate an excellent dinner, with the happiest, merriest party of Americans and Italians.
We were perched on the summit of a rise, full in
the sun, which neither umbrellas nor parasols
could render invincible, but we were so hungry
we didn't mind it.

Last of all, when the day was waning, came
the distribution of the prizes. The president,
glittering in golden armour, took his stand in the
centre, while one by one the victors approached
him—humbly kneeling as he presented to each

2*

crockery vases of various shapes and sizes, which
were received as treasures with delight and reverence, as also a draught of wine out of his
own peculiar flagon, which Ganymede had to
replenish very often that sultry day, I promise
you. As each successive victor retired, bearing
on high his earthen vessel, he was received with
loud and vociferous acclamations: deified Cæsar,
passing up the Forum and greeted by the assembled Quirites, was not more enthusiastically
cheered. There was a mock solemnity about the
whole scene that reminded one of enacted *tableaux
vivants* out of Cervantes; it was the heroic age of
knight-errantry admirably travestied and run mad.
The grave and majestic demeanour of the president, his eyes alone twinkling with suppressed
merriment, as he presented a crockery *scaldino* to
Shylock, victor in the donkey-race, and addressed
him in a speech of dignified eulogy on his gallant
achievement; the gibberish conversation between
himself and the Red Indian, the majestic and
solemn salutations exchanged with the ambassadors who advanced to take their leave, all was
perfectly in keeping—the sublime of the burlesque.
The beautiful "Am Rhein" was then sung in
parts, as none but Germans and enthusiasts *can*
sing it, the rocks and hills of the Campagna

echoing each long-drawn note of the rich Northern
melody. It still lingers in my ear; I think I hear
again the rise and fall of those many manly voices,
and see their upturned faces beaming with life,
and light, and energy, now deepening into one
overwhelming sentiment of national remembrance.
When it was all over the excitable Italians cried
"Bravi" like perfect demoniacs, and rent the very
air with their wild applause. The president, his
broad honest face flushed with emotion, then advanced into the centre of the throng, and with
outstretched arms, like a very pagan patriarch,
closed the rejoicings of the day by drinking one
long, grand, universal *lebehoch* (health) to all
languages, nations, people. "The entire world,"
exclaimed he, "I greet in this last loving cup!"
There was something catholic in this grand con-
vivial salute to the universe, and it reminded me
(not, as Hamlet says, "to speak it profanely")
of that thrilling scene by which the Roman
Church winds up its Easter rejoicings, when
the venerable pontiff, from the central balcony
of St. Peter's, with outstretched arms includes
all the nations of the earth in one solemn bene-
diction.

After such a soul-stirring finale to a happy
day, I returned home rejoicing to the eloquent

city that now, as ever, speaks with tongues of living fire to all hearts and sympathies, nourishing
in her mighty bosom art, genius, learning, and
religion.

CHAPTER II.

THERE is a lonely spot in the Campagna— lonely even for that desolate wilderness—situated in a bend of the river near the Ponte Nomentana, that most picturesque of all Roman bridges, with its castellated walls and towers engrafted on the solid masses of which it is formed. Weeping willows, and feathering pollards just bursting into the brightest tints of spring, sweep across the rapid stream flowing between high banks of grass carpeted with gayest flowers. Just beyond is a low, square-shaped mound, whose green sides are unbroken even by a furze-bush: that is the Mons Sacro, so celebrated in the republican annals as the spot where the commons, or *plebs*, retired on account of the great numbers confined for debt, until they were pacified and brought back to the

city by the consuls. To the left a lonely expanse, encircled by low hills, forms a natural
amphitheatre, the deep and rapid river dividing it
from the road; while farther on rises abruptly an
eminence once crowned by the well-known city
of Antemnæ, one of young Rome's bitterest rivals.
The sides of the encircling hills are broken by
patches of bright wheat, little dells shaded by low
copse-wood, and here and there a solitary watch-
tower.

I have visited that natural arena, singular for
its wild symmetry, when all nature has been
hushed; the only moving creatures being flights
of birds whirling round in giddy circles ere they
launch into the blue expanse—the only sound the
bleating of the goats, as they follow the shepherd
home to be milked—the only foreground objects
great flocks of sheep, with here and there a wild,
shaggy horse browsing or galloping at will. But
to-day "how altered was its sprightlier scene!"
for this same lonely spot is no other than the
race-course; and to-day is the "steeple-chase,"
and all Rome has turned out to see the fun.
Clouds of dust rising high in air indicate the road
from the great city, sending forth its immense
visitor and native population. Antiquity, and solitude, and contemplation are effectually put to the

rout. The bridges heavy with memories of Rome
—the old towers—the sacred mount—the hills—
all echo to the rattling, talking, laughing multitude.

A grand stand, ornamented with bright red
drapery, that told well among the universal shade
of emerald green, was erected under the hills, and
there the mass of the company gathered. I took
my stand on a rising ground commanding the
whole space, and found myself unexpectedly in
good company. The French ambassadress was
there in a picturesque riding-dress, reposing à la
Phillis on the grass, quite rural and touching to
behold, surrounded by a whole *état-major* of at-
tachés and officers, fancying themselves rustic for
the nonce. Well, there we stood, gentle and
simple, rich and poor, noble and plebeian, forming a diadem on that grassy mound, and all gazing on the animated scene below.

At certain distances along the course, which
extends about two miles, hurdles were erected;
and there was a low, artificial wall, and a deep
ditch which the people persisted in calling a *river*.
Even an Italian might have ventured those leaps;
but, considering discretion the better part of
valour, they abstained from taking any part in
such dangerous sport. Over the plain were scat-

tered innumerable groups; and there were hundreds of carriages, and those *toujours perdrix* officers—an indispensable ingredient of every Roman scene—the *carabinieri* keeping the course, and rushing violently about in pursuit of the unhappy and much-abused plebs. And there were fair equestrians, unmistakably Saxon, who condescended to curvet and canter in a show-off style quite refreshing to the *profanum vulgus*. Two knots of young priests clothed in scarlet (Greeks, I believe), not being allowed to descend among the mundane, stood on distant mounds, and grouped wonderfully well among the great universal ocean of green. Then there were contadine in picturesque dresses, and the poetical-looking beggars who sit for models and congregate on the steps of the Trinità di Monti; and vendors of drinks—*acque buone*—screaming; and coachmen swearing fine-sounding classic oaths —"By the body of Bacchus!"—and, altogether, such a pretty, animated, moving scene, that I quite despair of describing it.

The distant mountain-tops, still white with snow, melted lovingly into the fleecy clouds, leaving one in doubt which was land and which was vapour—lending a visionary and mystic frame to the prospect, and leading the mind away to un-

real worlds high up in the distant heavens, or to
the voiceless solitudes of primeval forests among
the Alban Hills.   How merrily the sun did shine,
making all nature glow and palpitate with renewed
life at the jocund burst of spring!

This season is the real summer of the Campagna, when the grass is green, the flowers blossoming, and the low trees in the damp dells
covered with leaves of a pale, delicate green.
When the great heats come, all is dried up as a
very potsherd, partaking of that burning tint that
strikes down from heavens of brass in arid, consuming heat—destructive to every living thing,
animate or inanimate.

By-and-by, after much waiting and grumbling,
out dashed the horses, with their pink, and red,
and yellow riders, scudding across the plain as
quick as the eye could follow.   Up and over they
go in a trice; the hurdles are cleared, and then
the ditch and the wall, clean and neat—quite
beautifully taken!   No, there is one brute that
will lag behind; and see! he won't leap that
sham little wall.   At length—see! they have all
arrived safe and sound; for to be sure they were
the very mildest of leaps, and the steeple-chase
was surely the most innocent affair in all sporting
annals.   Fame says a young Frenchman won;

and no great glory to him either.   But, the good
horses were English hunters—*cela se comprend*—
so, like dear brethren as we are, the glory of
victory was divided!

In a moment the pent-up crowd swells over the
plain in a moving mass, and we come down and
drive up and down on the smooth turf to see the
equipages and the people.

There is Torlonia in a high English curricle,
with two footmen in royal liveries behind him;
and there are Americans, with blue eyes and
Turkish beards; and English gentlemen in top-
boots, forgetting their *morgue*, and becoming quite
excited; and carriages full of smart wives and
daughters; and drags with six horses covered with
bells, and fur, and feathers; and Italian gentlemen,
very magnificent in gold chains and studs, with
wonderful trousers, mounted on miserable hacks:
and away we go towards home, into the mystery
of dust, flying mountains high before us.

I looked back, and already the lonely spot I
knew so well, cleared of the ephemeral crowd,
had returned to its loneliness.   The sun was now
sinking in purple and gold behind the mountains;
long, soft shadows were spreading over the plain;
down from the low hills crept the great flocks of
sheep, pressing on and on to their old pastures,

which the busy world had so lately usurped; the birds circled, and shot on "whirring wing" as before; and the cool evening breeze came laden with the scent of flowers and herbs, the frankincense Nature sends up to God's altar in the sky.

Tired of the dust, the noise, and turmoil of the Carnival, where men and women play at rude romps for a whole week, and do not even put an "antic disposition on" becomingly, I wandered up to the Capitol, and then down the steps on the other side, by the arch of Septimius Severus, to the church of Santa Martina, in a corner of the Forum. The day was cold and chill, but a warm sun fell on the steps leading to the portico of the church, where lounged all the beggars and idlers of the neighbourhood at full length—a motley assemblage of bronzed, half-naked savages, sullen-eyed and heavy-featured—clad in sheep-skin, the fur turned outwards.

The church of Santa Martina, although one of the oldest martyr-churches of Rome, has been entirely and ruthlessly modernised by Pietro di Cortona, who was so satisfied with his work of destruction that he called it "his daughter." When I say modernised, I mean made to look as lumberly and awkward as St. George's, Hanover Square. In form it is circular, with three principal altars. In a niche stands the original of Canova's "Religion"—a majestic figure richly draped, pointed flames forming a glory round the head. Near by is the picture of an obscure martyr who suffered under an imaginary Roman emperor; some one who had his hands and feet burned off, and was killed, but somehow came to life again, and painted a picture in the Lateran church, dying after all comfortably in his bed.

A flight of stairs mounting from the church conducts to the Accademia of San Luca, to which it was attached as a sanctuary. In modern times the name of Carlo Maratti is intimately connected with its increasing celebrity, he having been its president for many years. The gallery was icy cold, and I found the custode endeavouring to warm himself over a miserable *scaldino*. This old fellow was a great character.

"*Evviva*," said he, starting up as I appeared. "I am delighted to receive madama. Why was she not at the Corso, to see the *furore* of the Carnivale? That was strange, for ladies like fun —*ma, si vede bene*—the signora is a *dilettante*. Ah, *brava!* Now let us view the pictures, *che sono belli, bellissimi*."

He did not know half the masters, and those

he named were wrong; but there was no putting
him down.

"This," said he, "is a 'St. Jerome,' by
Titian. Ugh! *che colorito, un originale.* This is
Fiamingo——"

"Was it Rubens or Vandyke?" This question
he pretended not to hear.

"*Si, si—Fiamingo, ecco. Un originale proprio.*"

"What is that head?" said I.

"The Queen of England," replied he.

"Not the present one?"

"No, centuries back;" Elisabetta, he thought,
was her name. "*Non è bella,* but she was a fine
woman, and diverted herself in her day. *Si è
divertita immensamente, ma, poi!* Now the worms
would not feed on her. Pah!"

There was an exquisite "Venus," by Titian,
very little troubled by drapery, surveying herself
in a glass held by Cupid—a charmingly-coloured
work, the goddess radiant in the rich type of
Venetian beauty.

"*E bella,*" said the old fellow, scratching his
head, "*ma un po scoperta, ma! come si fa?* Nature made us all, and Eve wore no petticoats."

A young man, dressed in the romantic-Ger-
man-artist style, was standing by an easel, bearing

a copy of a most splendid "Claude," one of the gems of the gallery.

"*Ecco*," said he, "*questo signore*, he is come all the way from Genoa to copy our pictures, and it is so cold he can't work to-day."

"*Si, davvero troppo freddo*," replied the long-legged youth.

"He is the Marchese X——," whispered the old man; "*molto gran' signore, ugh! Nobilissimo*, but he loves the art, *che gli fa onore*."

"I cannot paint," chimed in the *sans-culotte* marchese, "it is too cold; *diantre! quel froid à cette saison!*"

There is much trash and many fine pictures in this collection, of which Murray says absolutely nothing. There is a splendid Titian, Diana bathing, surrounded by her nymphs, discovering Calisto, a group by no means *convenable* for the goddess of chastity; indeed, quite fit to figure on the walls of Fontainebleau in the time of Francis I. This picture was presented by a Russian, and when the Czar was in Rome the custode said he came to see it, and was very angry so fine a painting had been sent out of the kingdom. No wonder. It is superbly coloured, and leads one's thoughts away to the bright blue, dancing Adriatic, mirroring the snowy churches like great snowdrifts, within whose pillared sanctuaries such treasure-pictures are stored away. The old man grunted immensely over this picture.

"Ah!" said he at last, "it is dangerous to bathe sometimes—specially in company."

He seemed to have a malicious pleasure in informing me that the most *décolleté* pictures had been the donation of different popes; and as there are many of this description, I really am afraid the associates of San Luca have, notwithstanding their saintly patron, a terrible turn for the world, the flesh, and the devil.

One of the most beautiful *genre* pictures in Rome is here, by Guido Cagnacci, a pupil of Guido Reni's,—Lucretia with Sextus Tarquin holding a dagger over her. Suffice it to say that it is one of those remarkable works that stand out distinct when hundreds of others fade into the mist of memory. Copies of it are multiplied to an incredible extent; but it could not be hung up in a church, call it by any name you would. The picture tells the story, and tells it all too well.

"Ah!" said the custode, "Lucrezia was a fine woman for Tarquin's son to have lost Rome for her sake."

Sextus's face tells of love, despair, determina-

tion, rage, rapture—all mingled together in a
wonderful way. Those magic shades must have
come from Guido's own pencil. The so-called
picture of San Luca, said to be by Raphael, is
weak, mannered, and utterly deficient in grace.
San Luca, seated at an easel, is painting a portrait of the Madonna, who stands pushed *en profil*
in a corner, and of so plain and ordinary a *phy-
sique* that it is impossible Raphael could ever have
imagined such a creature; there is not one characteristic of his style. The painting is on wood,
and has been broken in two places. Of this work
Kugler says, authoritatively, that the head of San
Luca alone is executed by Raphael. When I told
the old custode this he became very indignant.

"What can books tell about it?" exclaimed
he. "All the world knows it is by Raphael. It
used to hang below, in the church, over the altar;
bestie di libri. Don't believe them, signora, I
beseech you. They only teach people lies. They
know nothing about it!"

There is a large "Venus and Cupid," by
Guercino, which the custode introduced to my
notice in these words:—

"*Ecco, Venere—con tutte le sue consolazioni!*"

I love Guercino and his inimitable *chiaro-oscuro*
and depth of shadow, contrasted and tempered

by a peculiar sweetness produced by the happiest combination of colour, though he *did* live in the time of the *Décadence*, and belonged to the Eclectic School.

Here also is Guido's "Fortune rising from the Globe," one of the finest frescoes in Rome—a glorious form—reminding one of the Rospigliosi "Aurora," with full rounded limbs, and matted yellow hair flying in the wind, by which Cupid holds fast as though determined to win and keep her. The *concetto* is most poetical, and the colouring perfect.

I have dwelt longer on this most varied and interesting collection from the fact of its being comparatively little known or appreciated. When I departed, the old custode doffed his weather-beaten hat, and bowing down to the ground, said—

"*Addio, cara signora;* I honour and respect you—*Stia buona bene e felice*—and remember the poor old fellow that keeps the *gloriosi quadri.*"

I wish to note down the traditionary footsteps of St. Peter and St. Paul at Rome, having visited the various spots connected with their supposed residence here with great interest. I have spoken of my descent into the Mamertine prisons, where for nine months they are said to have lain in

3 *

sight-seeing world go there to examine the painting by Sebastian del Piombo of Christ's flagella-
tion—a work, I confess, to my judgment, dark,
unintelligible, and unpleasing; a bad imitation of
Michel Angelo, who needed all his individual
genius and grandeur to make his contortions
bearable. No imitation of his style can ever
succeed.

In the cloister, whither we were led by a kind,
smiling monk, is a beautiful circular church—a
bijou of the Renaissance (very like in form that
temple introduced by Raphael in the background
of his cartoon of St. Paul preaching at Athens),
erected by Bramante over the exact spot marked
by tradition as that where St. Peter was crucified.

"*E proprio un miracolo,*" said the monk, "that
this church escaped, when the walls around it were
battered to the ground? *Si vede che qui sta il
santo.* He protected it."

It is divided into an upper and lower church.
In the latter is shown the aperture where the cross
was fixed on which St. Peter suffered with his
head downwards; thus nobly vindicating, at the
last moment, his love and devotion to the Saviour
he had once denied. A lamp burns before the
aperture. The monk put down a long reed and
brought up some of the golden sand from below,

presenting it to us as *una cosa di devozione*.   The
soil of the hill is in this part entirely of sand of
a particularly bright tint—hence the name of the
church, "Montorio"—or of the *golden mount*.

I must now take up the traditionary footsteps
of St. Paul from the same point as those of St.
Peter, namely, before his entrance into the Mamertine prisons.   On first arriving in the Eternal
City, St. Paul remained for two years, unmolested.
During that period he resided in a house situated
where now stands the church of Santa Maria, in
Via Lata, next door to the sumptuous palace of
the Dorias.   During this time he was only
guarded by one soldier, and from this retirement
he addressed his Epistle to the Hebrews, and
preached continually to all within his reach, Jews
as well as Gentiles.   St. Luke is said to have
borne him company, and under his dictation to
have written the Acts of the Apostles.

The present church is devoid of all save traditionary interest.   But there is a subterranean
chapel, containing three rooms (then on a level
with the city), which he is said to have inhabited,
with arched roofs, formed of great massive stones
rudely placed together, like the blocks forming
the Mamertine prisons.   Here, too, is also shown
a well, said to have sprung up miraculously, in

order that he might baptize those converted by his inspired preaching.

After the imprisonment of St. Paul and his separation from St. Peter, he was led on about three miles from Rome—on the Ostian Way—to a desolate place in the Campagna, where he was beheaded. Tradition asserts that his head, separated from the body, bounded three times from the violence of the blow, and that at each spot where it touched the ground a spring gushed forth. To commemorate this miracle a church was built at a very early period, and called San Paolo alle trè Fontane. I am always anxious to survey every place sanctified by tradition, however uncertain. It gives a local colouring and vitality to recollections beyond the perusal of a thousand books—making the events recorded, be they historical or religious, in a manner one's own. I therefore set forth, through the gate leading to the great basilica of San Paolo, on my pilgrimage.

After passing the huge church, we turned off from the great Ostian road a little to the left, up a steep ascent. Around, the low grassy undulations of the Campagna, now of a refreshing green, sloped down gradually towards a central valley or amphitheatre, where uprose three large their hunt. Although I am a born Englishwoman, I never knew to what a singularly remarkable and obstinate nation I belonged until I came into Italy. A wonderfully national nation are we, and therefore it is quite astonishing why people so satisfied and delighted with their own habits and customs should ever leave that all-perfect country they will insist on forcing everywhere.

But I have done, and I will go off and away up the long hill, winding round the sides of Monte Mario, crested by the Villa Mellini, and its groves of cypress, ilex, and pine—a very diadem of beauty—with the olive gardens nestling in the warm folds of the hillsides; and on and on by a long road, very dusty and very dull, until we reach a great green plain covered with grass, quite boundless to the eye—green below and blue above—nought save those two colours of primeval nature, the open Campagna.

Here, close by the road, which now becomes a grassy track, is a striped booth erected, fixed on one side to a large van, just like a show-caravan at a country fair; and round the little booth, which looks very solitary and odd, stuck up alone in that awful plain, are grouped beautiful hunters, sleek and satin-coated, pawing the ground, while others, with proudly curved necks

and flashing eyes, are galloping here and there
with their masters on their backs. Some are ridden
by fat English grooms, dressed quite *cap-à-pie*, talking cockney as they congregate together. Red coat
after red coat trots up, and carriage after carriage
full of pretty ladies, but quite properly and sufficiently distant in their looks to make it certain
that they are English bred and born; and then
last of all come the two whippers-in and dogs,
nice sagacious creatures, which quietly lie down
to rest and husband their strength until the right
moment comes—and then we shall see. The
wind blows fresh from the glorious mountains
skirting that boundless plain, and one begins to
wish the red coats would leave off hanging over
the carriages and entertaining the *belles* within—
because it is growing cold—when, just at the
right moment, we are off. On go the dogs, and
the horses and riders, and a little man on a
rough pony, with a hatchet to *cut through the
hedges* (hear this, O ye of Melton Mowbray and
the Warwick Hunt!), because the infant hunt is
too weak to leap much; and after come the carriages in a long file, driving out, as it were, to
sea on the trackless waves of that placid ocean
of grass. There was no road, and we bumped
up and down on the inequalities of the grass in a

most comical fashion. The hunt crept slowly on
seeking for a fox they could not find. On they
went, forming the prettiest tableaux imaginable,
down into narrow valleys, damp and dewy and
emerald green, their sides clothed with low-tufted
woods and luxuriant sedges—now hiding, now
displaying the persevering red coats—standing
some above, on the brow of the little rising hills;
others below, winding in the sinuosities of the
glades far onwards.

We in the carriages quietly followed the noise-
less search after a fox that would *not* be found,
and, mile after mile, crept on up little rises, and
down into gentle dales, in the most singular drive
I ever took in all my life. Every now and then
I thought we must be overturned; but not a bit
of it. One carriage ventured, and the rest followed like a flock of obedient sheep. The breezes,
fragrant with the rich odour of herbs and flowers,
swept softly around; broad shadows formed
gigantic shapes on the grass; flocks of small
birds rose, and dispersed at our approach; and
the sallow, skin-clad *pastori*, mounted on shaggy
ponies, or leaning on long staffs, came forth to
stare at the *élite* of the great city below.

The scene, though moving, was silent; voices
were lost on that great hunting-ground; the val-

leys still bent onwards, and led us enticingly
away, away, far out into an unreal and dreamy
world. By this time I had almost forgotten why
we were there, and neither cared for nor heeded
what was passing around. I desired to return,
and so we hoisted sail and steered towards the
huge dome rising so strangely out of nothing,
like a great balloon sailing in a firmament of
green. As we proceeded, the sheep in their folds
started up and stared at the unusual invasion, and
the *pastori* rested on their poles, gazing sadly
upon us. Had it not been for them we never
should have landed on the road.

When I look back on those hours spent on
the boundless Campagna prairie, it comes before
me like a vision, and the hunt and the silent procession like phantasmagoria, perfect and beautiful,
but shadowy, soulless, and unreal—forms conjured up from the deep recesses of those enchanted valleys to lead one on, ever wandering,
like the vague and endless strivings of a dream.

We returned as the sun was setting, and I am
much inclined to believe those spirits melted away
and vanished in the long shadows of coming
night, and that ourselves were the only living
beings who returned to the great city.

*   *   *   *   *

When the Holy Father Sixtus, the second of that name, pope and martyr, was dragged to the stake by command of the Emperor Valerian, a young priest, of gentle and engaging aspect, followed him, and thus addressed him:—

"Father, whither are you going without your son and your deacon? Never before were you wont to offer sacrifice without me. Have I been wanting in my duty? Have I displeased you? Try me, and see if I am not capable of enduring torments, fire, or imprisonment for the sake of our Lord."

"I do not leave you, my son," replied the venerable pontiff, moved at the youth's generous impatience for the rack and the flames of martyrdom; "my spirit shall watch over *you*, who are reserved for a greater and more glorious trial than is vouchsafed to *me*. In three days we shall meet in heaven!"

Then the young priest rejoiced to hear that he should be so soon with God, and, like a traveller disposing himself for a long journey, prepared all his worldly affairs, distributed his scanty means to the Christian poor, who bathed with their tears the deep-hidden altars in the mysterious catacombs, where the holy sacrifice was offered. His proceedings were not so well hidden but that the Roman prefect got word of them, and, in high rage, sent for the young priest, and desired to be shown his hidden treasures.

"Bring to light," cried he, "those vessels of gold and candlesticks of silver you possess. They are wanted for the altars of the gods. Render also to Cæsar the things which are his; he needs the coin for the maintenance of his armies. Your God certainly coined no money on earth, and needs none now he is dead. Words alone were his revenues; keep thou them and give the gold to Imperial Cæsar."

The young priest, nothing daunted, replied:—

"You say the truth; the Church indeed is rich in inestimable treasure. I will make out instantly an inventory, and display to you all our possessions."

Then the young priest went round to all the holes and corners of the city: he sought in the sand-pits of the Esquiline (where herded the slaves who were branded, and the vile murderers escaped from justice) for the persecuted Christians, who were happy if there they might burrow like beasts, so that they had but peace. He went into foul holes and noisome courts—to the close-packed houses under the Tarpeian Rock—to the poor huts beyond the Quintilian meadows—and he as-

sembled at length all the Christian poor—maimed,
deaf, and blind—in a certain spot on the Cœlian
Hill, together with the lepers, and the poor virgins, and orphans, and widows. He then went
to the prefect, and told him to come, for the
treasure was spread forth.

When the luxurious prefect, fresh from the
scented waters of the marble baths, came among
such a loathsome throng, he gathered up the folds
of his toga, and burst forth in a great rage:—

"By the eternal Jove! I will teach you to
mock me! How dare you, base Christian, to
bandy pleasantries with me? What means this
abject crowd?"

"Why are you displeased?" rejoined the young
priest, unmoved by his rage. "It is gold that is
low, vile, and mean, and incites men to violence.
We have none, we despise it. You asked for the
treasure of the Christian Church—lo! it is before
you—the sick, the weak, the wretched, they are
Christ's jewels, and with them He makes up his
crown! I have none other."

Then the prefect grew more furious.

"Do you presume still to mock me?" cried
he. "Have the axes, and the fasces, and the
sacred eagles no power? In your vanity and
your folly you desire to die the same vile death

4 *

as Jesus; but new tortures shall be invented—death shall be to you the sweetest boon."

Then the prefect commanded his lictors to make ready a great gridiron, and to cast under it live coals nearly extinguished, that they might slowly burn; and Lawrence—for he was the courageous young priest—was stripped, and bound, and extended on the gridiron, until his flesh was slowly burnt off his bones; he all the while continuing in earnest prayer, and imploring the Divine mercy on his native Rome, and that, for the sake of his sufferings, the Christian faith might be planted there. So he died; and his remains were carried without the city to the Veran field, beside the road leading to Tibur.

In after years, when Constantine the Emperor had seen the glorious cross hanging in the blue sky over the Monte Mario, where he lay encamped against Maxentius, and had been converted, and had proclaimed Christianity the religion of the universe in the great hall of the Ulpian Basilica, he bethought him of this glorious martyr, and built a church over his tomb.

I quitted the city by the Porta San Lorenzo, anciently called Tiburtina, with its two antique towers, twin sisters of decay, and its long links of aqueducts stretching far away into the plain.

About a mile distant, on a dusty road now leading to modern Tivoli, the basilica appears rising out of solitary fields.

The portico, running the entire length of the front, might, except for the six Ionic columns—pilfered from some pagan temple—serve as the entrance to a large barn.   Bare wooden rafters support it; and the walls are covered with fiery frescoes, quite smelling of brimstone and an un-utterable place below.   These atrocities are said to have been executed in the time of Pope Hono-rius III.   I need not add that art was then almost at its dying gasp, weighed down under the in-fluence of the dark ages.   Here is the soul of St. Lawrence, represented as weighed on a balance by black fiends; the coronation of Peter Courte-nay, as Emperor of the East, which took place in this basilica; dead men raised to life; souls rescued from purgatory by the Pope flying up to heaven —all wild, indescribable scenes, and represented in the stiffest forms of Byzantine pattern.

The interior is of majestic proportions, every way worthy of the proud name of Basilica; but nevertheless there is a bare look about it, in spite of much magnificent decoration.   The nave is supported by Ionic columns of classical workman-

ship, but the entablature is only whitewash, while
the old wooden ceiling, carved in high relief, is
infinitely rich, and coloured of a pale blue. The
floor is *opus Alexandrinum.* The two ambones,
or marble pulpits, from which were read the Gospel
and the Epistle, have been spared, and are of
rare beauty, ornamented with large slabs of rich
red and green marbles, with mosaic borders of
even more precious materials. The whole of the
apsis, or tribune, considerably raised by marble
steps, is supported by twelve magnificent pavonaz-
zetto columns, all, save two, decorated with graceful Corinthian capitals. Unfortunately they are
half sunk to accommodate the elevation of the
tribune; their proportions can, therefore, only be
judged of from below. Above is an arched gallery, supported by smaller columns. This forest-
like mass of pillars, arches, and capitals, all of
exquisite workmánship, produces a fine effect.
Old frescoes ornament the vault of the tribune,
mosaics decorate the arch. Under the high altar
is a subterranean chamber, or "confession," visible
from above, where lie enshrined the bones of St.
Stephen and St. Lawrence. These remains are
approached by Catholics with extreme awe, for,
when restorations were going on in the church,
in the reign of Pelagius II., the marble sepulchres

being opened, and the bones irreverently touched, all present died within ten days.

As I stood leaning against a pillar on the high-altar, I could not but feel penetrated by the solitude and singularity of the scene—the heavy damps of ages, the solemn traditions of the martyred dead breathed from these stern old walls. Not a sound was heard from the outward world; through a side door the sun streamed in from a spacious cloister, surrounded by columned arcades —all solitary, silent, forsaken.

I had had a fancy to visit the shrine, from a most singular tradition attached to it.   In the reign of Pope Alexander II., about the time that the Normans invaded England, there lived in the convent a pious monk, who was so fervent in prayer that he invariably rose before daybreak to invoke the intercession of the holy martyrs, whose remains lie under the altar.

Once—it was a Wednesday in August—while kneeling there, he saw, with his open eyes, just as the daylight began to glimmer, the great doors open as of themselves, and a stately man, with a long beard, enter, habited for the performance of mass, accompanied by a deacon of a youthful and pleasant aspect, followed by a crowd of many soldiers, monks, and nobles, all in strange attire.

Although a numerous retinue, their footsteps raised
no echo—the church was as quiet as when the
monk prayed alone. Astonished at the strange
sight, he rose from his knees trembling, and as
the procession silently advanced up the nave, he
hid himself behind a pillar and watched. As
they approached the high-altar the monk softly
approached the young priest (for his mind mis-
gave him, and he was very curious, though sorely
frightened), and, with much respect, whispered to
him in these words:—

"I pray you tell me who are you that prepare
with such solemnity for the morning mass?"

The youth with the pleasant aspect replied:—

"The one habited as a priest is St. Peter. I
am Lawrence. On the anniversary of the day
when our blessed Lord was betrayed by the
wicked Judas's kiss, and when the judges ap-
pointed that he should expire by the slow torture
of the accursed tree, I also suffered martyrdom
for his love; therefore, in memory of that day,
we are come to celebrate the solemnity in this
church built over my bones. St. Stephen is also
among this blessed company; the ministers are
angels of paradise; and the others are apostles,
martyrs, and confessors who have all sealed their
faith with their blood. They have had in re-

membrance the day of my death, and because it
should be known of all and honoured to the glory
of our Lord in the universal church, I have desired
that you should see us with your mortal eyes, that
you should make manifest this solemnity to all
men. I therefore command you, when day breaks,
go to the Pope, and tell him from me to come
here quickly with all his clergy, and to offer up
the blessed sacrifice for the people."

"But," returned the monk, now pale with awe
and fright, as he saw the visionary multitude
gathering round him, and felt the icy chill of their
garments, "but how shall I, a poor monk, make
the Pope believe my words if I have no sign of
the holy vision?"

Then the young saint took off the cincture
with which he was girded, and gave it to the
monk, to show in token of all he had seen. The
monk, being full of fear, returned to the monastery,
and, as the day was now broke, assembled the
brethren, told them of the vision, and showed
them the cincture. Then all, knowing the holiness of the monk, believed his words, and went
with him to the Pope, who then dwelt at the
Lateran Palace, on the Cœlian Hill, and he, after
assembling the conclave of cardinals, gave great
thanks to God and the holy St. Lawrence, and

celebrated solemn mass at the church, which is
repeated every year. This, therefore, causes much
fervour to St. Lawrence, and induces crowds to
go on a certain Wednesday in August to venerate
his remains.

Beyond the church of San Sebastiano, the
Appian Way extends in a straight line to the
tomb of Cecilia Metella, about a quarter of a mile
distant, which stands crowning a rugged eminence,
"firm as a fortress with its fence of stone." Turning to the left, in a large park-like expanse of
the finest turf, one of the rarest prospects of old
Rome opens before one. It is enchanting! How
shall I describe it? I will try.

At my feet lies a mass of majestic ruins, at
first confused and undefined, but by-and-by the
long lines of walls, the turrets, and porticoes
range themselves into symmetry and order, as
under the touch of a fairy's wand, and I see the
great circus of Romulus stretching in two long
parallel lines before me to the length of 892 feet,
a mighty enclosure, narrow in breadth, with turreted towers at the extremity near which I stand.
Beyond are the walls of another square enclosure,
supposed to be the stables of a riding-school connected with the circus. There are the marks of

arches still engraven on the great outer walls, which alone remain.

Above, the ground rises in a gentle swell, covered with vines and pale mystic olive trees, perhaps the most appropriate shade Nature ever devised to overshadow the ruins of the past. On the edge of the hill stands the church of San Sebastiano, and a dark cypress grove, while among the olive-grounds appear no less than three separate temples and porticoes. I know of no scene in or near Rome as satisfying to the mind as this little-frequented spot, where so much remains to tell of the grandeur of ancient Rome.

Following the line of the hill, beyond the olives and their accompanying vineyards, comes a soft picturesque plantation of feathery elms, standing out alone on the great background of the open Campagna, undulating here in endless inequalities of rounded hills and gently-sloping valleys, spanned by the majestic line of the Claudian aqueduct, marching, as it were, in an ever-advancing procession towards the Eternal City.

Above rise pale outlines of mountains and the rounded summits of the Sabine and Alban Hills, now, as the sun is sinking resplendent with delicate shades of pale pink and purple, melting into the blue vault of heaven in charming gradations of

colour.   Here and there a white mass—Frascati
or Tivoli, or the great convent, once the temple
of Jupiter Latialis, on the summit of Monte Cavo
—catches the lateral rays of the sinking sun, and
shines out in dazzling whiteness.

I wandered on over the smooth green sward
to rising hillocks opposite, on a level with the
great round tomb of Cecilia Metella.   Here Rome
itself burst on my sight, with its walls and domes,
turrets and spires, never more beautiful than when
seen from this side, softened by foreground and
foliage, and backed by the wooded slopes of
Monte Mario and the steep Janiculum.

Around me fed an immense flock of sheep,
spreading themselves over the classic meadow; a
herd-boy, with the brigand-pointed hat and gay-
coloured girdle peculiar to the Campagna, sat
upon a stone and watched the sheep and me.
The vast mausoleum frowned down on me, flanked
by its turreted walls, erected by the Gaetani in
the middle ages, when this solid structure was
transformed into a fortress.   These walls have in
their turn become ruins, adding to, rather than
detracting from, the dignity of the tomb they en-
shrine.   I suppose no one ever visited this monument without mental questionings in some sort

similar to those so gracefully expressed by Byron
—to end, as did his, in this simple fact—

> "That Metella died.
> The wealthiest Roman's wife :
> Behold his love or pride!"

The ivy and trailing plants that now diadem
the summit of this magnificent monument were
fanned by the soft evening breeze. No sound
was there to awake the remarkable echo which
accurately repeats all sounds intrusted to it, so
that when Crassus mourned the loss of "that lady
of the dead," the funeral solemnities must have
been infinitely multiplied by endless repetitions of
the wailings of the mourners, as if the infernal
gods themselves and all the souls in the nether
Hades had united in one vast chorus of groans
and cries to bewail the deceased Cecilia. It seems
strange that after the lapse of so many ages, the
same echo which repeated the lamentations for
the wife of the Roman senator, "so honoured and
conspicuous," should remain to serve with "damn-
able iteration" the impatience of every cockney
visitor. That echo, too, must have borne many
a rough message in the mediæval days when this
tomb-fortress was besieged by the Connétable de
Bourbon, who opened his trenches before the
Aurelian wall and the Street of Tombs as re-

morselessly as though these venerable remains boasted not a single recollection. Fortunately for me, the present was tranquil as the past; silence reigned supreme.

I next descended into the arena of the circus of Romulus immediately beneath, through one of the ruined towers flanking its extremity. The interior, carpeted with brightest grass, is luxuriant in vegetation; whole gardens of variegated flowers, the wallflower, ivy, and low plants of ilex tufted the ruined walls, clothing their nakedness with the rich colouring of returning spring. A peasant was gathering fennel, and immediately approached, begging me, for the love of Heaven *"e per le lagrime della Madonna,"* to assist him, and pointing to the scanty herbs which he had so carefully collected, in order to make into *minestra*, or broth; "for," said he, "we are starving in the city, and I am come out here to gather a few herbs, to us most precious."

It is from the well-defined remains of this circus, so much more perfect than any similar structure, that antiquarians collect their actual knowledge of the arrangements. It was first supposed to be the circus of Caracalla, and is so named by the accurate Eustace; but later excavations made by the Duke Bracciano, brother of

Torlonia, to whom the ground belongs, prove from inscriptions that it was erected to Romulus, the son of Maxentius, A.D. 311. From its admirable preservation, extreme beauty of position, and the poetry and interest of the ruins around it, this circus may be considered as unique among the remains of ancient Rome. The external walls are almost unbroken; in many places the vault supporting the seats still remains; the foundations of the two obelisks, terminating either extremity of the spina (running lengthwise through the circus, and forming the goals), still exist; and on one side stands a sort of tower where the judges sat. Near where I entered is a gallery, which contained a band of musicians, flanked by the towers I have mentioned, whence the signal for starting was given.

There were seven ranges of seats, containing upwards of twenty thousand spectators, and the extreme length of the circus was 1,006 feet. The chariots passed round the spina, and the most fearful accidents constantly occurred from the rapid driving, the narrowness of the space, and the jostling permitted, as also from the fact of the reins being fastened round the bodies of the charioteers. A large gate is found near the spot where they started, used only for the removal of

the bodies of those killed in these encounters, as
the ancients deemed it a most portentous omen
to pass a gate defiled by the passage of a dead
body.

I studied the place till my imagination built
up the ruins and filled the vast arena with spectators. I fancied the solemn procession advancing
before the commencement of the games, headed
by the emperor, seated on a superb car. Troops
of young boys follow, and escort the charioteers
driving the chariots destined for the race, some
harnessed with two, some with four, and even six
horses. Then come the athletes, almost naked,
followed by troops of dancers, consisting of men,
youths, and children, habited in scarlet tunics, and
wearing a short sword and a helmet ornamented
with feathers. They execute war-dances as they
advance to the sound of flutes, and harps of ivory,
and lutes. Hideous satyrs covered with the skins
of animals, over-grown Silenuses, with all kinds
of monsters in strange travesties, imitate with
various contortions the more dignified dancers
who precede them, seeking to divert the spectators by their extravagance.

Then appear a troop of priests, bearing in
their hands vessels of gold and silver containing
incense, perfuming the air as they advance. Their

approach is heralded by a band of music. Others
bear the statues of the gods, who in honour of
the occasion condescend to leave their temples.
Some deities are borne in splendid cars enriched
with precious stones; others, too sacred for the
eyes of the *profanum vulgus*, are enshrouded in
close litters; they are escorted by the patricians,
and nobly-born children are proud to hold the
bridle of the horses that draw them. The procession makes the circuit of the assembly, and is
received with general acclamations, especially on
the appearance of any idol particularly venerated
by the credulous plebs. The statues are then
placed in a temple on cushions of the richest
materials. The emperor, descending from his
chariot, pours out libations—the earthly Jupiter
to his heavenly brother. The games are then
proclaimed, and the chariots of green, blue,
white, and red emerge from *carceri* and rush on
their furious course, as a white cloth, thrown
from the imperial gallery, gives the signal to
begin.

There is a melancholy charm, a silent though
eloquent language of the past, interwoven with
these ruins (now warmed and tinged by the bright
sun into a ruddy brown), inexpressibly enticing.
It is a sheltered, sequestered spot to while away

the twilight hours, on the soft banks of grass under the shadow of the high walls, and surrender oneself up to fast-flitting fancies. I seated myself on the capital of a fallen pillar, among the long grass and waving reeds. The arches, the pillars, the towers, the ruined temples peeping out of the olive wood on the hill above, all spoke out plainly their sepulchral language; and the dark cypresses beside the catacomb church whispered also as the breeze moaned through their heavy branches.

I at length reluctantly withdrew, passing under the triumphal arch at the opposite extremity of the circus through which the victorious charioteers drove amidst the shouts and acclamations of the multitude. That ruined arch now abuts on a road leading to Albano; but time would not permit me, on that occasion, to proceed farther.

CHAPTER III.

The Carnival—The Valley and Fountain of Egeria—Society and the
Artist World.

I LOVE the Eternal City, after my fashion,
with a devotion as unquestioning and entire as
ever animated the bosom of an ancient Roman;
but I am bound to confess that there is one
period when Rome is most unacceptable—during
the Carnival. A perfectly contagious plague of
folly, vulgarity, license, noise, and ribaldry is
abroad, and I would desire to retire from all
possible contact with the incongruous scene.
Solemn, grave, meditative Rome, with its dim
memories looming through the chasm of bygone
ages, its frowning palaces, its deeply-shadowed
cavernous streets, its classical population (wanting
only the toga to make proper senators), its religious
displays, pious associations, popes, cardinals,
churches, ruins, relics, palaces, sculptures, and
mosaics, given up for ten days to vulgar common-
place tomfoolery! Oh, horrible! May I never see

5*

"the Niobe of nations" so debase herself again!
It was to me the most profoundly melancholy
period of my stay, and I only went into the
Corso to be able, from actual seeing, the more
heartily to abuse the degrading scenes there enacted.

Elsewhere the Carnival may be very amusing
in picturesque bright Italy, where the very beggars
wear their gaudy rags with a kind of royal dignity,
but it is utterly unsuitable to the grandeur of the
Eternal City, and ought to be discontinued by
general acclamation. If the Carnival, and the
English, and the Codini were banished from
Rome, there would remain nothing "to fright it
from its propriety."

During the latter days of the Carnival, from
two till six, all the world rushes madly to the
Corso, now fluttering with flags, tapestry, and
banners, while red and white hangings picturesquely drape the galleries, terraces, cornices, and
windows of the stern old palaces "of other days,"
until their familiar faces become quite unrecognis-
able; for though masks were denied to the people,
the houses certainly are allowed to adopt them.
People are crushed into carriages and cars by
dozens; streets overflow; the windows are crammed;
the galleries and verandahs tremble with the

weight; the dust flies like sand on the desert; the
sun shines too hot; the wind blows too chill; and
after all this *chiasso*, "what come they out for to
see?" A few dozen miserable ragamuffins of the
lowest grade in dirty costumes hired in miserable
slop-shops (for none but the lowest ever dream
of a regular costume)—crowds of the refuse of a
great city—troops of half-tipsy and much-excited
soldiers—gentlemen with a charming return to in-
fantine simplicity, dressed in "over-all" pinafores
of brown holland; and ladies wearing blue wire
masks, which make them look particularly hideous.
Then one is pelted with black and dirty flowers,
and blinded with showers of lime (the *gesso* of
the studios put to such unholy abuses!) which
every rascal may freely fling in one's face, and
which descends also in deluges from above, making one's eyes intolerable for days (mine positively ache to write of it), screamed at, sworn at,
stared at, by a vast crowd, where one recognises
not a soul, so muffled up is every one in the
aforesaid wire masks, veils, and great hats of the
conspirator cut—all this martyrdom being occasionally rewarded by a tiny bag of sugar-plums
thrown by a compassionate male friend, or a
bouquet of decent flowers, which is either lost in
the street, or the next instant torn violently from

one's grasp by a vile little street urchin, who
makes a few *bajocchi* by its speedy sale!

The enormities committed by the ladies and
gentlemen placed in the galleries are utterly out-
rageous and unaccountable; it is a serious, solemn
system of folly unrelieved by any excuse of fun
or frolic—a so-styled farce, without laugh or jest.
English, and Germans, and Americans there take
their stand with all the grave reserve of the sober
nations of the North, and, from buckets filled
with lime and baskets of unpleasant little musty
bouquets, alternately shovel out bushels of lime,
or pelt with faded flowers the crowd beneath,
looking as composed and serious as if fulfilling
some religious penance. Sure such a travestie of
mirth never was beheld! The Italians *have* some
fun about them, and play the harlequin like gentlemen; but the others!

The ancient Romans marked their season of
Feriæ by universal peace, happiness, and liberty.
Slaves were manumitted, and masters waited on
their servants at the feast; and doubtless they
would thus have handed down the tradition to
their descendants, had not the Christian strangers
of modern days, called by the Romans "barba-
rians," misapplied and abused the once genial
and classic games in honour of the god Saturn,

who in the golden age ruled with his wife Astræa,
or Justice, over the tribes of ancient Latium, and
was worshipped in his lofty temple on the Capi-
toline Mount.

It was cold and disagreeably windy weather,
and clouds of white dust strewed the streets, the
houses, the carriages, poisoned the air, and clung
to one's clothes, and face, and hair. The roars,
the cries, the screams, the rush and roll of a great
multitude, made it a scene of perplexity, an-
noyance, and discomfort not to be described. No
one laughed—no one joked amid this Babel; it
was noise without mirth, romping without play.
I was inexpressibly disappointed and disgusted.

At five o'clock the Corso is cleared; and after
the *carabinieri* have properly persecuted and
annoyed the crowd, in order to make room, eight
or ten riderless horses, covered with jingling
chains and little sharp-pointed stars and triangles
of gilt metal, rush or dawdle along according to
their private feelings at the time, like runaway
beasts that no one will take the trouble to catch.
These miserable apologies are called the *Barberi*,
because Arabian horses used to run here in the
good old times; but nothing now remains of the
Arabians except their name, as it is yet commemorated in a street called the "Ripresa dei Bar-

bari," where they are caught after accomplishing their dismal career.

This contemptible wind-up to the day's weariness is wretched beyond description. I thought of Ascot and Epsom, and the noble satin-coated steeds scarcely touching mother-earth in their giddy flight across the great heathery commons, and I could scarcely believe the scraggy animals which had just passed were of the same race. Each day I returned home from the Corso more weary and fatigued—a moving mass of white dust, sitting knee-deep in dirty bouquets and *débris* of *confetti*.

The only part of the Carnival that moved me with a sensation of enjoyment was the night of the "*Moccoli*." Dark-winged benignant night wrapped the flaunting scene in her sable mantle, harmonising the incongruous groups into broad masses. The hum of the multitude, united and softened by the gloom, rose up like a vast chorus of rejoicing; the ribald jest, the insolent attack, was mitigated as the lights came out by millions, above, below, around—"whiter than new snow on the raven's back," as Juliet says—a universe of bright twinkling stars. On the windows of the palaces, along the roofs, in the balconies, there were lights—myriads of lights; while below, every

creature among those moving thousands carried
his or her taper—sometimes a whole bunch—
dancing and dashing to and fro in the dark
streets like planets fallen from their spheres, and
fairly gone mad. After a time the glittering mass
resolved itself into what appeared the deep precipitous sides of a mighty cavern, blazing with
countless flames that ebbed to and fro in the
evening breeze like waves of gems rising to meet
the heavens. Meanwhile, the moon, pale and
subdued, shone serenely in a softened atmosphere
of blue.

The fun waxed fast and furious during the
two hours' duration of this grand and dazzling
pageant; but to my mind it was more subdued
and chastened to the humanities of life than the
charivari of the day. Those who merely looked
on like myself, and bore no *moccolo*, were let
alone and unmolested, or only saluted with now
and then a long doleful cry of " *Vergogna, vergogna, senza moccolo, senza moccolo-o-o*"—a kind
of indignant wail in accents of infinite disgust—
or a sharp "*Come, signora! senza moccolo, par impossible—è pazza!*" from some pert youth, who,
finding his reproaches ineffectual, walked scorn-
fully away, brandishing his light vigorously to assault a more congenial stranger.

The showers of lime and the bouquets had now vanished, all being intent on the exquisite fun of extinguishing each other's taper. And fun there was—real good living fun, not at all of the drawing-room sort—uproarious tumult, universal deafening noise, fighting, screaming, laughing, and struggling—men scuffling over the expiring remnants of a light, women stretching half over the balconies and struggling out of carriages after obstinate tapers held securely on high; whilst, lo! from behind—thump!—it is gone; and the cry, "*Senza moccoli!*" rings out, and then all separate in chase of new fun, and are instantly re-engaged, fighting hard as ever. "*Moccoli, morte a chi non porta moccoli!*" sounds again; men rush hither and thither, carrying torches, paper lanterns, and pyramids of light, dancing to and fro on long poles, until the cry becomes like the watchword of a general conflagration.

Along the street there were windows and doors full of merry Roman girls—jolly, rollicking grisettes!—mad with fun and laughter, holding high above their heads the fated *moccoli*, which crowds of gallants were endeavouring by indescribable feats to extinguish. How they did laugh!—it was delicious! They were always at the same game whenever we passed, and would

be at it now had the bell not sounded at eight
o'clock—that horrid bell—when all the world is
driven away, and the last *moccolo* is blown out by
those disagreeable *carabinieri*, who seem to have
a wicked spite against the mirth in which they
cannot join.

And so it is over, and Rome quiet. The
hosts of strangers are gone, disappearing in great
machines dragged by strings of horses to the
station; and the streets are silent, and the carriages no longer lined with white to save them
from the showers of *confetti;* and I am truly glad,
and never wish to see Rome desecrated by the
Carnival again.

I now resume my account of that portion of
ancient Rome in the vicinity of the tomb of Cecilia Metella. On returning a few days afterwards,
I passed through the circus of Romulus, out by
the ruined Arch of Triumph on the Albano road,
and found myself in a feathering grove of elm
trees, fringing the inequalities of the Campagna.
The perfume of violets blossoming in the fine
herbage scented the refreshing breeze, and swept
over the verdant , expanse, singularly and most
picturesquely broken by ruins—here, a temple;
there, a ruined portico; near by, a wall over-
mantled by ivy—all serving to mark the rise and

fall of the ground, backed by the Claudian aqueducts on one side, while on the other Rome herself, plainly defined, crowned the Cœlian and
Esquiline Hills.   Nature and art combined to
form a scene of Arcadian beauty and Palladian
grandeur; the past, the present, and the future
were visible to the reflective eye; the broad
heavens overshadowed all; and the setting sun,
that eye of the universe, gave the final touch to
the harmonious unity of this sublime picture.

I strolled on through the open wood towards
the small ruined church of St. Urbano alla Caffa-
rella, once a temple of classic beauty, dedicated,
it is said, to Bacchus, whose picturesque worship
was especially suited to these wild idyllic solitudes,
where the sighing of the wind across the Campagna might be mistaken for Pan with his reedy
pipes wooing some coy nymph; or where the
summer breeze might whisper the voice of Zephyr
as he approached the chariot of the light-footed
Iris; or where the deep shadows in the clustered
trees resolve themselves into the forms of dryads
and hamadryads, half hidden in green leaves
beside clear brooks whose bubbling waters sparkle
on the flowery turf.   It is easy even now to trans-
form every ruder sound into the discordant laugh
of a satyr or a mocking faun; to people the

valleys with green-haired nereids, and to believe that a spirit or a god appears in the grotesque contortions of the gnarled trees around. Solitude feeds these fancies. I was alone, and gave free rein to my imagination; built up every ruined altar and decaying temple whose ruins now strew that verdant plain; filled the portico of Bacchus' ancient fane with worshippers; crowned the hills with glowing Bacchantes, torch in hand, ready to celebrate the Brumalia with shouts and cries as they bear aloft the golden image of the god crowned with vine-leaves and purple grapes. I pictured, too, those pure and poetic existences of 'the "graceful superstition" of old, the nymphs, whose haunts were in the wooded dale or piny mountain, "in forests by slow stream or pebbly spring, in chasms and watery depths," dividing under their gentle sway all the realms of Nature.

But to resume. I now had reached the temple of Bacchus, barbarously disfigured by being converted into a church, which has in its turn become a ruin. Below the decaying altar a dark door leads down into the catacombs, which extend even to this distance into the Campagna; but the door has been closed ever since a party of young collegians, attended by their tutors, were lost in the gloomy passages. Below the temple, or church, the ground rapidly sinks into a deep and narrow valley, enclosed by soft rounded hills, at whose base runs a stream—the Almo, I believe. Immediately opposite is a dark grove of ilex trees, circular in shape, still called "*Il bosco sacro*," one of those spots anciently consecrated by solemn pagan ceremonies, where the Gods revealed prophetic secrets to the priest or priestess of the neighbouring temple.

Descending into the dell, and passing to the left under the hill, I reached a deep grotto, overshadowed by fluttering aspen, feathering ash, long trailing garlands of fresh May, yellow broom, and luxuriant weeds, which beautified and concealed the ruins to which they clung. The sides of the grotto are covered with moss, the slabs along the floor are slippery with the same verdant carpet, and there is a bubbling of waters with a fresh earthy smell of spring and flowers, which is perfectly delicious. The grotto is entirely uncovered, the sides are walled, and at the lower end, under a solid arch, lies the mutilated statue of a recumbent nymph, buried in ivy, once that "Egeria, the sweet creation of some heart which found no mutual resting-place." For I was now standing within the sacred precincts of Egeria's retreat; and the "cave-guarded" spring that gushed from beneath the statue, and found its way into the valley along little stone-conduits bordering the walls, is said, by tradition, to be the very rill beside whose running waters Numa met his goddess and his love. Antiquarians assure us that it is not so, and that tradition has no right to appropriate this sweet spot consecrated by Nature to the sylvan deities; but I love to go in a believing spirit, and to accept the beauty, actual and suggestive, around me.

A tradition so replete with beauty, a spot so exquisitely romantic, are subjects too ideal and delicate to endure the rough handling of antiquarian critics. I do not desire their lore. I will only listen to the bubbling of that sparkling little streams as it dances forth through the moss and the weeds into the valley beyond. Juvenal is said, in classical days, to have angrily lamented that the walls of the grotto were plated with rich marbles, and the fountain artificially decorated. His ire might be now appeased, for it has returned to its pristine state of solitude and simplicity—the grassy margin and the naked rock. The marble linings, the pillars, the statues, have disappeared; and Nature alone adorns the monument of the past. Egeria herself is now but a mutilated torso!

Of all the legends of infant Rome none is more poetical than the story of Numa and his goddess-wife Egeria, who descended from her place among the gods to inspire him with wisdom and counsel. Tradition says that after living some years with his first wife Tatia, the daughter of Tatius, co-sovereign with Romulus of yet unbuilt Rome, he became a widower, and was chosen to govern the growing state founded on the Seven Hills. It was then that Egeria came to his aid, and in those mysterious meetings under the sacred grove beside the little streamlet dictated that code of just and wise laws which the Roman people so prized and loved.

But, alas! Numa was not always faithful to his spirit-bride. Egeria had rivals of her own incorporeal and mystic nature, for Numa met also the Muses in these nocturnal interviews, and boasted that he was specially distinguished by one *Tacita*, the Muse of Silence, to whom he erected temples. But his gentle love, Egeria—his tried and constant friend—was not to be disheartened: she loved him to the end, and we shall find her again among the classic shades of Nemi proving her love in death.

There is an extraordinary mysticism mixed up in the character of Numa, full of graceful interest

and incident—his love for Egeria, her vale, her
grotto with its sparkling rill, his meetings with the
Muses, and the stange story told by Plutarch of
his interview with Jupiter.   When the Aventine
was neither enclosed nor inhabited, and abounded
with fresh springs and shady groves haunted by
satyrs and fauns, Numa mixed the fountain where
they drank with honey and wine, and thus intoxi-
cated and caught them.   They in their rage quitted
their natural forms and assumed many dreadful
and fearful shapes, but finding that their arts could
not prevail to frighten Numa and induce him to
break their bonds, they consented to reveal to
him the secrets of futurity, and ended by bringing
down Jupiter from heaven to discourse with him.
"But," says the story quaintly, "it was Egeria
who taught Numa to manage the matter, and to
send away even Jupiter himself propitious."

Standing musing under the shade of the
sacred grotto, I had well-nigh forgot another ruin
near at hand, also furnishing a world of recollections.   I wandered along the valley in search of
it, and came upon the ruins of a brick temple on
the border of the river—small, indeed, but well
proportioned—said to be dedicated to the god
Rediculus, who prompted Hannibal, when lying
there encamped, to retreat from Rome.   But this

tradition yields to another yet more interesting, which declares it to be the identical fane erected in honour of Fortuna Muliebris on the spot where Coriolanus met his wife and mother, and was prevailed on by their entreaties to draw off his army from Rome. What reader of Shakespeare does not recall that sublime scene where Coriolanus, surrounded by the tents of the assembled Volscians, advances to great Volumnia and Virgilia in these words?—

> "My wife comes foremost; then the honour'd mould
> Wherein this trunk was framed, and in her hand
> The grandchild to her blood. But, out, affection!
> All bond and privilege of nature, break!
> .   .   .   .   I melt, and am not
> Of stronger earth than others."

I reascended the steep hill to the temple of Bacchus, feeling that I had pondered over a delicious page in the annals of the magic past.

There are cliques and sets at Rome, more varied and antagonistic in character than are often to be found in much larger and more populous cities. I have belonged a little to all, entirely to none. There is the ecclesiastical set, composed of cardinals, monsignori, and high dignitaries of the Church—very slow, pompous, and humdrum indeed, dreaming away their lives in the discharge of various pious duties, and hun-

dreds of years behind the busy, bustling life of
the North, where climate and habits perpetually
drive people onwards as if the very furies pursued
them. They lazily drive about to each other's
palazzi in big red coaches drawn by black horses,
with a retinue of antiquated retainers in the most
singular liveries, coats hanging down to their
heels, and cocked-hats on their heads. Within
sit the starch, solemn old gentlemen in purple
and red, their pale parchment countenances never
relaxing into a smile.

Once past the city gates, it is "their custom
of an afternoon" to descend and walk slowly
along the dusty roads between high walls which
entirely obscure the prospect, attended by their
extraordinary retainers, who look antique enough
to have handed Mrs. Noah into the ark. Most
courteously do these princes of the Church salute
all who pass them; and there were two or three
whom I well know by sight, from my admiration
of their holy and benevolent countenances. Now
and then these "grave and reverend signiors"
give a reception, when some female relation of
high degree receives the guests and does the
honours. The Holy Father himself leaves the
Vatican occasionally by one of the gates for his
trottata, generally dressed in white, and wearing

6*

a broad hat of red silk.   Then it is etiquette for
every passer-by to go on his knees in the dust
and receive the Papal blessing, rendered doubly
valuable by the benignant grace with which it is
bestowed.   But since "the evil days" of his flight
and the siege, no welcome or applause ever greets
his presence.

It is a ridiculous and idle prejudice for people
to talk and write about the immorality of the
Roman clergy; such nonsense can only proceed
from the pens of ignorant, prejudiced, and evil-
minded persons.

The higher ranks of the Romish clergy are
remarkable for their moral conduct, serious demeanour, and blameless lives.   It is most rare
indeed to hear in any direction of the slightest
légèreté, and when it is detected it is remorselessly and unhesitatingly punished.   A certain
monsignore gave scandal this winter by a too
mundane and vain conduct and deportment, without, I believe, much, if any, criminality.   He was
at once degraded in the face of all Rome.   The
cardinals are occasionally present in general society—in rooms where there is no dancing, but
their manners are so reserved and distant (except
to particular male friends) that they can scarcely
be reckoned among the company.   The parish

priests of Rome are generally a most active and excellent body of men, irreproachable in conduct, and, but for the unhappy political dissensions which divide from them the sympathies of the people, would be justly and sincerely beloved. It is extremely rare to hear a whisper of any misconduct among the religious houses of either sex. When discovered, it is uncompromisingly punished.

But to return to my immediate topic—Society. There is the set of Roman princesses, grand, haughty dames, proud of their descent from the Cornelias, the Lucretias, and the Portias of the republic. They are, as a body, remarkable for correct conduct, extreme devotion, and a lamentable want of intellectual cultivation. I believe many a raw English school-girl is better acquainted with Roman history than these princesses, born and reared amid the imposing ruins of the city of the Cæsars. They dislike strangers unless especially introduced—particularly Protestants, who are not considered Christians—and clan and club together in a *noli me tangere* spirit very unusual among the Italians, who are in general an easy, hospitable, polite, and facile people. But the Romans generally, and especially the princes and princesses, are remarkable for their senseless pride.

They are unceasingly haunted by the notion of
their descent from the Fabiuses, the Maximuses,
and Cæsars of old, and endeavour, very unsuccess-
fully, to ape the dignified and solemn bearing
of those ancient pillars of the state—a proceeding
absolutely ridiculous in the degenerate state of
Rome in the nineteenth century.

As to the ladies—my special province—one
must forgive them their foolish arrogance when
one sees the superb palaces, the magnificent and
glittering saloons they inhabit; the trains of retainers and servants that crowd their halls, and
wait on their slightest caprice. From infancy
they are nurtured with a luxury, and looked on
by their inferiors with a devoted respect and
veneration, quite sufficient to turn wiser brains,
and confuse more expanded intellects. Each lady
has her own *entourage* and circle—clients like the
followers of the ancient senators; and although
her palace may occasionally be opened for a
grand ball to the *profanum vulgus*, the magnificent mistress, her debt to popularity once paid,
speedily closes her doors and retires to enjoy her
morgue and her nineteen bosom friends, washing
her princely hands from all further contamination
with the common or unclean.

Then there is the diplomatic set, of necessity

more hospitable and affable *outwardly*, but in reality excessively exclusive. Each ambassadress forms a little court of her own, composed principally of her compatriots, the *état-major* of his excellency, and some distinguished hangers-on. Among these ladies are some women of intellect, wit, and beauty.

Then there is the American set, a numerous body, extremely sociable, and remarkable for general intelligence, bustle, and go-ahead propensities, and for the fragile and delicate beauty of the younger ladies—those pale daughters of the New World, whose alabaster skins, melting blue eyes, and flaxen hair are nowhere more conspicuous than among the olive-complexioned, black-eyed, luscious beauties of the South.

There is also a learned set at Rome, necessarily cosmopolitan, but decidedly Catholic; and there is a rabidly Protestant set, which considers the Pope the abomination of desolation, and have been heard to stigmatise his blessing as a curse. It is wonderful they ever trust themselves within the walls of Babylon, for the spirit of the place can never visit them. Then there is that awful amalgamation of dissipation, riches, scandal, and exclusiveness, the English set, who have appropriated to themselves an entire quarter of the city,

comprising the beautiful Pincian, where they have
their English shops, English prices, books, papers,
servants, and *cuisine*. They live much together,
sharing only in the grand festivities of the Roman
nobles and the diplomatic corps. They are a
powerful faction, and are constantly endeavouring
to Anglicise Rome by dint of money and over-
bearing arrogance. They picnic in solemn temples,
and underground in dim and dreary baths; drink
champagne among moss-grown tombs; ride donkeys to Hannibal's camp; get up horse and
hurdle races over the consecrated soil of the classic Campagna; light up the Coliseum with blue
and red lights; sit on camp-stools in St. Peter's;
and invade every gallery, palace, or monument
with the Saxon tongue and Saxon ill-breeding.
Those who wish fairly to judge of Rome proper
should "stay over the season," and see the English all out, in order to understand how much
they have spoilt it. They give no end of balls
and suppers, dance in Lent when they dare, turn
their backs on the Pope, ridicule the Catholics,
talk shocking scandal—which the Italians *never*
do—and spend oceans of money, causing Rome,
at this moment, to be the dearest residence on
the Continent.

Last of all, there is the artist world at Rome—

a merry, genial, cosmopolitan throng, compounded
of French, Italians, Germans, Swiss, English, and
Americans—a jovial, many-hued company, boast-
ing names that make one's soul thrill at the remembrance of the immortal works they are handing
down to posterity.   Yes, I love the artist world at
Rome, and am proud to reckon some of its world-
wide names among my friends:—Gibson, now,
alas! gone—who, in his life, so identified himself
with Greek art and Greek sculpture that he seemed
to have acquired the calm repose, the dignity, and
the wisdom of an ancient philosopher.   Who that
ever really knew Gibson did not admire his simple,
amiable nature and high-minded rectitude of
character?   He was at once the most modest and
the most unflinching of men; pleased with the
simplest meed of sincere praise, yet regardless of
the opinion of the whole world if to obtain its
applause he was obliged to compromise his artistic creed, the religion of his soul.   A mind of
this temper would have been great in any walk
of life.

Then there was Crawford, the American sculptor, whose gallery still remains; whilst among the
living are Story and Dessoulavy, Rogers and Tilten,
and Miss Hosmer, the loved pupil of Gibson, and
Page, and Shakespeare Wood—Americans all but

the last named. Nor must I forget Penry Williams,
the greatest of English painters at Rome—com-
bining the dewy softness of Constable, the clear,
brilliant tone of Callcott, with a purity of style
and absolute perfection of colouring all his own.

A great name, too, is that of Tenerani, the
head of the modern Italian school, to be judged
of in his noble works—uniting the force and
grandeur of Thorwaldsen to the grace of Canova.

There are life and vitality yet in the modern
Italian school, spite of much feebleness and affec-
tation, as must be allowed when contemplating
Tenerani's immortal work, "The Angel of the Resurrection"—perhaps the most sublime effort of
modern sculpture. Then there was Overbeck, a
monkish old man, who lived shut up in the grim
old Cenci Palace in the filthy Ghetto—a man so
silent, of aspect so uninviting, and with manners
so austere, that one never could believe him capable of creating those virgins, angels, and glori-
fied spirits of ideal purity, breathing the very airs
of Paradise. Cornelius also, that great father of
modern German painting, long lived on the summit of the Pincian in the very house where, thirty
years ago, he, in conjunction with Schadow and
Overbeck, determined to break the bonds of custom,
and first dreamt of, and then achieved, the revival

of fresco-painting, now, by their works at Düssel-
dorf and Munich, spread over all Europe. The
walls of this house are still decorated by their first
efforts, which, with some crudeness and inex-
perience in the use of a novel material, indicate
uncommon and unusual power. Riedel too, that
wonderful master of the German school who still
lives, and who lights up his nymphs with beams
as it were snatched from the living sunshine; and
Mayer, and Coleman, the Paul Potter of our century; and many other rising geniuses among the
younger artists; for I have but named the *dictators*
in the republic of art of the present century. But
I must stop, for in these recollections of the artist
world of Rome my pen runs riot with pleasant
memories.

CHAPTER IV.

A Classical Excursion to Albano and Nemi, intended for those fond of
the History of the Past.

WE started four in number—a delightful party
—on a fine, fresh, sunshiny morning in "the merrie
month of May," for Albano. We were all well acquainted—and the gay jest and the piquant re-
joinder went gaily round. We laughed at each
other, at ourselves, at all the world, going forth
into the Campagna through the heavy portal of
San Giovanni Laterano, jealously guarded by
carabinieri.

Our party consisted of very various elements.
There was an elderly friend acting duenna to our
wilder spirits; calm, pleased, silent herself, but
ready to share in the mirth of others. There was
one highly gifted, my friend H——ns, the son of
a poetess, a poet himself, an antiquarian, an
historian, a theologian—nothing came amiss to
his well-stored mind; each stone had for him its
suggestive interest, every monument its eloquent

history, every lovely phase of Nature its idyl. Art and antiquity through his mouth became simultaneously articulate. I always said, if the dry bones of "Murray's Guide" could be vivified, animated, and clothed in less "dry-as-dust" garments, the result would be H——ns, the most instructive compendium and agreeable companion that ever turned over the moss-grown remains of antiquity. Our *third* was S. W——, a sculptor, looking for *form* in all things, and disdaining colour and gradations of shade as things of nought, full of his art and of the antique, and withal eminently good-natured and obliging. As for the fourth, so delicate a subject as a description of myself cannot be expected. I cannot take my own portrait, as the painters did in the Florence gallery of celebrated artists, looking into a glass; for where can I find a mental mirror, "showing the inmost part," by which to draw myself? I must leave my readers to make their own sketch of me, first imploring their good offices not to paint me too black.

Well, on we rattled along the paved road, traversing the Campagna *dans tous les sens*, as the French have it. Nowhere, I believe, in the world does one drive out into a perfect wilderness, devoid of houses or inhabitants, on a paved road, rough and jolting as the high street of a country town, except in this singular and exceptional place. A few miles and we were sailing along on the waving expanse of that grassy ocean, the turf bright as unset emeralds, its uniform colour broken by unenclosed fields of corn, with here and there tufts of luxuriant poppies, broad tracts of yellow buttercups, great staring daisies, and sweet violets. To the left lay the solemn lines of the Augustan aqueducts, linking the Alban Hills, and the pure springs that rise in their deep bosoms, to the service of that queen of cities reposing yonder on her seven-hilled throne. Each arch forms as it were a separate picture, presenting new scenes of beauty—a gallery as unique as it is singular.

Beyond the fair face of Nature nothing arrested our attention for some miles. To the right was the distant outline of the Street of Tombs, mound after mound of dark ruins marking the successive monuments. A mass of ruins, void and without form, close on the Appian Way, was pointed out by H——ns as *Roma Vecchia*, so named because the contadini firmly believe this to have been the site of the ancient city, the why or the wherefore being utterly obscure. It was probably a temple or a villa bordering the "Viarum Regina," along whose pavement the chariots and the horsemen went and came, thick as the falling leaves in an autumnal gale.

We came at length to the foot of the Alban Hills, which rise abruptly from the plain. Before ascending, the modern road is joined by the old Appian Way, which shoots forth out of the city through the Porta San Sebastiano, straight as an arrow launched from a bow. If we had had eyes sufficiently long-sighted, we might have seen the sentinel keeping guard over the crumbling arch of Drusus.

Where the ancient and the modern roads unite is a wretched tumble-down wayside *osteria*, called Frattocchie — a cut-throat-looking place enough—redolent of fleas, sour wine, dirt, and bad smells, especially by reason of its *cucina cucinante*, in which garlic would decidedly pre-dominate. H——ns here stopped the carriage, not from any uncharitable purpose of condemning us to eat in such a hole, but to call our attention to the spot as being the supposed site of Clodius's murder by Milo, the friend of Cicero, whom he chose for his advocate on his trial for the murder. But Cicero arriving at the Forum in a litter, and seeing the space filled with soldiers under arms, and Pompey himself seated on high as president, was so confounded and terrified that he could scarcely give audible utterance to, that celebrated discourse, "Pro Milone," which would alone have immortalised his eloquence.

H——ns recalled our early recollections of that most fascinating of books next to the Arabian Nights, Plutarch's Lives. "It chanced," said he, "unfortunately, that Milo, going to Lanuvium to consecrate a priest, met Clodius, surrounded by his clients and retainers, on this spot, where then stood a temple to the Bona Dea. Milo was quietly reposing in his coach, like a luxurious Roman gentleman, in company with his wife Fausta, the daughter of Sylla; but, as in the later mediæval days of Montagues and Capulets, the servants of either party took up the well-known feud of their masters, and commenced fighting. One of the servants of Milo pierced Clodius's shoulder, and Milo, considering that if Clodius survived he would eternally devote him and his house to the furies of revenge, ordered his attendants to finish him. And so fell Clodius."

We drove on, rejoicing in the knowledge we were thus pleasantly picking up like flowers along the hedge-rows, and began to mount the hill at a slow pace.

The road was bordered on the left by low rocky banks, with here and there a mass of ruins

or a group of great spreading pine trees, whose
sharp lines cut against the radiant sky with the
full force of Italian contrast.   Flowers wreathed
many-coloured garlands over the reddish rock;
little green lizards rushed to and fro amid perfumed blossoms; gay butterflies fluttered; and spring
birds sang an audible chorus of jocund spring.
A little shrine to the Madonna was cut out of the
tufa rock, and decorated with flowers; a lamp
burned before her image, which was enclosed in
a glass case; in front kneeled a contadina in the
pretty costume of the country, with rich red
folds falling from her head over a shawl of white
muslin.

To the right lay vineyards and gardens, looking like gigantic patches of basket-work from the
yellow *canne*, or reeds, to which the young vines
and just opening plants were trained; olives waved
their pale, shadowless boughs among the vineyards, spreading their fresh, whitish leaves towards the sun.   Here and there a valley sank
deep down, and a stream rushed away in the
direction of the Campagna, tumbling over great
masses of rock, and cooling the air around.   This
was the near view.

Behind lay the Queen of Capitals—her domes,
towers, spires, and walls thickening on the low

hills far away—vast, shadowy, dreamy—melting into the azure haze of distance.

The rich and many-tinted wilderness, on whose soil uprose the cities of Latium, spread around in its vast length and breadth; while to the far right a long monotonous line marked the shore towards Ostia and Antium (Porto d'Anzio), with the Tyrrhene Sea visible beyond all, a sheet of burnished gold. There was immensity in that view, suggestive of chaos and eternity. The land ran into the glistening sea undefined, and the mountains melted into the clouds, knitting the elements together in one great mystic whole around the Eternal City throned on those blue hills! What takes me a certain time to write I drank in with a few delicious glances. However, it was soon over, and we had now approached within sight of Albano, scarcely to be perceived until one is under its gateway. As to the lake, so utterly invisible is it from this side, that one would be ready to venture one's life that no lake nearer than Thrasymene existed.

To the left, close on a cluster of villas standing in rich orange and lemon groves, at the entrance to Albano, stand the massive ruins of a tomb, second only in size to that of Cecilia Metella, once encased with white marble, now but a mere mound of crumbling brickwork, crowned with a perfect diadem of plants, shrubs, and grasses. That tomb, H——ns informed us (and so do the guide-books, only they want his pleasant, well-turned sentences and interesting details, giving as 'twere the day and hour), was now admitted on all hands to be the resting-place of Pompey's ashes, borne by the hands of his second wife, Cornelia, from Egypt, she never resting until she had deposited the monumental urn within sight of the city over which he had ruled, and where men had surnamed him "the Great."

Pompey, defeated in the final struggle at Pharsalia, fled to his fond and faithful Cornelia, who fainted as she heard of his mischance. Together in one Seleucian galley they sought the hospitality of Ptolemy, King of Egypt, at Pelusium; for Pompey, Roman though he was, could not bring himself to ask safety and mercy at the hands of conquering Cæsar. A council was called among the Egyptians, and it was resolved that Pompey must perish, on the mean principle of subserviency to Cæsar. He was brought from the ship where he had left Cornelia, whose eye followed his every motion, suspicious of the event. She saw him seat himself in the little craft—a fishing-boat—and take out to read a speech he had prepared to address to Ptolemy. As the boat approached the shore, hope shot into her sinking heart. A crowd of persons advanced (as she thought to do him honour), but at the moment when, stepping from the boat, he placed his foot on shore, a base assassin came from behind and stabbed him in the back. She saw him fall, like an ancient Roman, covering his face in his mantle, and she saw no more. She too fell, and a shriek so piercing rent the air, that it reached the cruel group gathered about the dying hero.

"That shriek," said H——ns, "chronicled by Plutarch, has come down to us sharp and clear through accumulated centuries. I never pass that grey ruin without picturing to myself the stately Roman matron landing at Antium, followed by a long train of mourners and retainers—pale and worn, yet dignified, shrouded in her mourning robes—bearing the urn containing the ashes of her husband to this very spot, on his broad lands near ancient Alba."

The modern town of Albano is as ugly a place as I would *not* wish to see, consisting of one long street, where everybody can see everybody else, a great deal of dust, some tawdry shops, and two tolerable hotels—which to me, however, would be unbearable, because standing

in the centre of the town. I had pictured to myself an elegant, classic Locanda on the borders of
the lake, overshadowed by evergreen woods. To
be sure there are the very pretty gardens of the
Villa Doria, always deliciously cool and shady,
and at all hours hospitably thrown open to the
public—a favour the more to be esteemed as the
family spend there a portion of every autumn.
The site of Alba Longa, however, must not be
sought for in the modern town, but in a quite
different situation. We drove through the long
street out on the further side of Albano: still no
signs of lake, not even a *soupçon* of where a lake
might be. As we descended a steep hill through
rocky banks overshadowed by trees, the country
looked wild and pretty, tossed about in a picturesque manner.

Close on the gates of Albano, towards Ariccia,
on the brow of a descent, H——ns called our
attention to a most remarkable tomb—a square
mass of majestic proportions surmounted by four
low obelisks at the corners, with a pedestal in the
centre. Two of the obelisks have disappeared,
and the summit has become quite a little grove
of low shrubs and young trees and creepers.
H——ns laughed at the idea of this tomb being
the burying-place of the Horatii and Curiatii, as

has been affirmed. Their celebrated conflict took
place much nearer Rome. "There is no doubt,"
he said, "that it was of Etruscan workmanship,
and erected to Aruns, son of Porsenna;" that same
king we all know so well, from Macaulay's spirited
lines beginning—

> "Lars Porsenna of Clusium by the nine gods he swore,
>   That the great house of Tarquin should suffer wrong no more."

On a precipitous hill opposite, and about a
mile distant from Albano, the small town, or
almost village, of Ariccia crowns the height. Between lies a deep valley, but the twin hills of
Ariccia and Albano are linked together by a
stupendous viaduct, at least one hundred and
fifty feet high, with four or five rows of open
arches; a most striking achievement of the late
Papal Government, by which, at an immense cost,
it was erected.

It is wonderful to see Ariccia such a vulgar,
dirty, modern little place, and to think that it has
been sung by Horace and Virgil, and chronicled
by Livy and Plutarch, none of whose writings
will certainly gain in pleasing associations by a
near knowledge of it as it is. There is a miserable inn, to which strangers resort during the
malaria season in Rome. We left the carriage
and walked along the road, crossing the viaduct,

and admiring the fine views over the Campagna, the sea, and the vast unfathomable woods; but we could still not discern a trace of the cosy Alban Lake, whose waters are so deeply buried under the overshadowing hills.

On leaving Ariccia, another valley intervenes between it and an adjacent height half a mile off, on which Genzano, whither we were bound, is situated. We had now penetrated into the deep primeval woods of aged oaks, chestnuts, gnarled ash, and elm, that clothe the lower portion of the Alban Mountains as with a great mantle, the entire range ending in the elevated summit of Monte Cavo, now conspicuous to our left, and crowned by a white-walled convent. This convent occupies the site of what was once the temple of Jupiter Latialis, built by Tarquin the Proud as the solemn gathering-place of the forty-seven cities of the Latin Confederation — a splendid position, commanding the entire land from Soracte to Antium. "No profane hand," said H——ns (who had become more and more eloquent and interesting as we advanced further and further into the classic scenes of Rome's early history), "dared to desecrate or injure that sacred shrine, the renowned scene of the Feriæ Latinæ, endeared to the superstitious remembrance of all Latium, where Julius Cæsar had celebrated his triumph as dictator, and thousands of less illustrious generals enjoyed the honours of the Ovation. Even in the beginning of the last century ruins remained, stupendous enough to mark the temple's original size and magnitude; but they were all destroyed and appropriated by Cardinal York, the last of the Stuarts, for the purpose of erecting that hideous Passionist convent now visible like a white spot on the summit. Ruins, marbles, columns, statues, all were ruthlessly swept away, leaving the consecrated site of Rome's early triumphs without a vestige of the past—an act of destruction the more extraordinary, as the reigning pontiff, Pius VI., both understood and admired art and antiquity. All that now remains is the old Via Sacra, vestiges of which are to be still traced through the chestnut woods on the face of the mountain opposite Rome, in the direction of Rocca di Papa."

The venerable primeval forests that surround Genzano and Ariccia are exquisite. Fine single trees stand forth in grassy openings, where early spring flowers of those bright hues peculiar to the South spring out of the moss-grown rocks that break the surface of the ground in picturesque confusion. Here and there the wood deepens under a lower growth of ilex, laurel, box, and arbutus, their dark boughs lending a mystic character to a sylvan region.

Here Numa wandered in retired and secret places, haunted by the nymphs whose soft voices he loved. Here of old dwelt Zephyr and Echo, and here murmured many a trickling stream. We had no time to dwell on these bewitching memories, but proceeded along a magnificent terrace— once the Appian Way, now the high road from Rome to Naples — and thundered through a splendid avenue of fine old trees, called the Olmata, leading into the small town or *paese* of Genzano, the last of those attractive outskirts of Rome to which its inhabitants escape during the dangerous summer heats.

"Look," said H——ns, "at that round hill just in advance of the town and nearer the plain, covered by vineyards, and crowned by a mediæval tower. That is said to be the site of ancient Corioli, whither Coriolanus fled when exiled from Rome. From thence he issued, leading the Volscian forces against his native city; and there he returned when, overcome by the entreaties of his mother and wife, he withdrew from the siege. No ruins remain of the ancient city where the Roman general ended his days. Some say that

he was murdered by the Volscians out of resentment at his conduct—others that he lived to be
an old man, and was heard often to complain
'that the evils of exile bore much heavier on the
aged.' Pliny says that even in his day no traces
of Corioli were visible. The hill is now called
Monte Giove."

Genzano consists of one broad street on the
declivity of a hill. Below are hills crowned with
feudal castles, remnants of the middle-age dominion of the stout Roman barons, now ruined and
romantic adjuncts to a landscape both grand and
beautiful. The valleys lead down into the vast
expanse of the outlying Campagna, encircled by
a shining fringe of gold—the suggestive Mediterranean, along whose unruffled and tideless shores
many a white-sailed ship was visible.

By the time we had reached Genzano we were
just in that state of mind and body proper to the
appreciation of a good dinner. Even our poet so
far descended from his Parnassian heights as to
express the pleasure he felt that our long fast was
to be broken.

We were received by a most kind and hospitable host, whose *casa* is the only decent residence
within the precincts of Genzano, by name Jacobini,
nephew to the late minister of finance. When

the Italians *are* hospitable and cordial, the Red
Indians themselves cannot exceed the heartiness
of their welcome, the boundlessness of their household generosity. Jacobini's face beamed with
genuine delight as he conducted us up long
flights of stairs to the *piano-nobile* of his house,
near where the swallows build their nests—the
modern Italians and the birds having a decided
simpatia for an elevated situation just under the
eaves. The Queen of Sheba was not received
by King Solomon, in all his glory, with more
empressement than we were: the best chambers
were opened—the hospitable board spread by an
old contadina, wearing a red petticoat edged with
green, a green bodice laced with red, bows of
the same colour as shoulder-knots, a lace apron
and tucker, and yards of snow-white dimity stowed
away in mysterious folds about her almost hairless
head. Great gold earrings and a large brooch
completed her attire. Round the room in which
our refection was served hung four portraits of
lovely girls—one too many for the Graces.

"Ah!" said Jacobini, "those are the pictures
of my sisters—*mie care sorelline.* When they were
all unmarried we had a happy home. I loved
them well; but they are all married now. She
with the red rose in her hair, the best, the pret-

tiest, went last — *e adesso son solo!*" and he sighed.

H——ns whispered to me he should like to write a sonnet on that sweet beauty-sister, who never would grow old or faded, either she or the rose in her hair, under their glass frame, whatever the original might do.

S. W—— remarked, what a lovely bust she would make.

But Jacobini looked pained, and changed the conversation, saying—

"*Oh Dio, quanto è cambiata adesso, povera mia Rosa tanto amata!*"

But there was no time for sadness; for the soup, or *minestra*, now appeared under the beneficent auspices of the *donna di faccenda*, who, in her red petticoat, skipped about with the agility of a young *ballarina*. Then came a huge bowl of *such* macaroni, with savoury sauce—such macaroni as only Italians know how to prepare; and three dishes of roast and boiled meat, and delicious *frittura*, light and airy as crisp snow on the highest mountains, and piles of savoury *salamè*, and ham and salad, and sweets and fruit —*such* a dinner, which, truth to say, we required not the hospitable pressing of Jacobini largely to

enjoy! Bottle after bottle of wine was produced,
the corks flying pell-mell around. This was the
vino sincero of Genzano, famous for its vineyards
—a wine to be drunk in tumblers (like strong
sweet cider in taste). Then came sherry and
claret, and Heaven knows what other beverages.
I began to tremble at last for the heads of Poetry
and Sculpture, who were obliged perforce to par-
take of all, no refusal being permitted by Signor
Jacobini, whose broad face grew redder and fuller
with every bottle. By the time dinner was over,
we were all the most warm and cordial friends
that ever sacrificed to Bacchus under the classic
shadow of Monte Cavo. We were to remain for
a week?—No, we couldn't. For the night?—No,
a thousand thanks, it was impossible; the strong
walls of Rome would not contain our agonised
and expectant families did we not return that
night. "*Ma supplico loro, mi facciano la compia-
cenza, il gran favore,*" &c., &c. Well, we came
then to a compromise; we would return and spend
another day, and eat another dinner—(small blame
to us for the same); so the worthy Jacobini, who
had eaten, drunk, and talked like ten ordinary
men, was appeased; and we broke up, to view
under his chaperonage the classic beauties of the
Lake of Nemi, which, like its sister of Albano,

lies so hidden that not a glimpse had we of its existence, although positively *on* its shores. At the top of its straggling street an imposing old palace obtrudes its gloomy, heavy front between us and the green woods around, belonging to the Duca Cesarini, an Italian magnifico married to an English lady. Passing along another of those grand leafy avenues, or galleries surrounding Genzano, whose overarching branches formed a long-drawn aisle of that mighty cathedral whose roof is heaven, we reached a gate leading into the recesses of the duchessa's garden.

Elysium itself, I do not believe could be more wondrously fair than were those scented groves encircling the Lake of Nemi. The lake itself opens before us as a secluded, unruffled expanse, five miles in circumference. Its waters are of a peculiarly deep green, reflected from the overshadowing woods, now bursting into the brilliant colours of spring. A more romantic, lonely little tarn, embosomed in silent hills which dimple around it like the leaves of a gigantic lily—the waters its cup-like petal—never opened to human eye. The spirit and worship of the old gods of Greece seem still to cling to these once consecrated groves, and to recall dim visions of those days when the gods loved to descend from high

Olympus to drink the new wines of the vintage, and dally with the fair daughters of earth.

Jacobini — dear, good-natured creature! — neither caring for nor remembering the classicalities, dragged us about to admire fountains flinging waters into marble basins, which flashed back in stars and irises; swans reposing under willows in little emerald islands; and countless camellia trees, whose waxen flowers of red and white blushed forth from thickets of shining leaves. He then led us by long galleries of verdure, formed of laurel, ilex, and other dark and fragrant trees, down towards the lake, through a woody labyrinth of paths.

All at once I missed H——ns, and as I wanted to hear all his lore, I anxiously hunted him out. He was at last discovered seated, book in hand, in a delicious arbour of flowering oleanders. To our question, "What he was reading?" he replied, "Byron, of course;" and then and there repeated these lines, which we heard on the very spot with renewed and particular pleasure:—

> "Lo, Nemi! navelled in the wooded hills
> So far, that the uprooting wind which tears
> The oak from its foundation, and which spills
> The ocean o'er its boundary, and bears
> Its foam against the skies, reluctant spares
> The oval mirror of thy glassy lake."

Poor Jacobini looked terribly bored at our enthusiasm, to him utterly incomprehensible, and begged some of the party to descend through the winding paths to the edge of the lake. I preferred remaining to hear H——ns discourse upon the many graceful mythological legends which lend such a charm to these now desolate shores.

Opposite to where we sat, sheltered from the heat by an overhanging *berceau*, appeared the very picturesque village of Nemi, half-way up on the hillside. H——ns said that there were near it some ·vestiges of a temple, supposed to have been dedicated to the Ephesian Diana, to whose worship all the woods bordering the lake were dedicated. Here Diana was worshipped, together with Hippolytus, the unhappy son of Theseus by his first queen. Racine has immortalised his story in noble verse, and Rachel, as Phèdre, has in her turn immortalised Racine by her magnificent acting.

To this temple Iphigenia, with her brother Orestes and his friend Pylades, escaped from Tauris, carrying with them the statue of Diana, which the Delphian Oracle had commanded the wretched Orestes to transport there, so that under the shade of these sacred woods his wearied spirit might find repose.

In these groves the nymph Egeria wandered
when death separated her from Numa, her human
lover.   Inconsolable for his loss, she woke the
echoes by her lamentations, and fed the flowers
with her tears, until all-merciful Diana, pitying
her grief, changed her into a fountain, which still
trickles down into the lake near by the village,
on the site of "Glorious Diana's fane."   Within
such groves, and beside such a tranquil lake,
Actæon perhaps might have gazed—with that fatal
curiosity which cost him so dear—on the fair
form of the cháste goddess while she bathed in
these placid waters.   Here, on clear summer nights,
when the amorous breath of Zephyr alone fanned
the breeze, and Boreas and his band were deep
buried in Ocean's caves, Diana may have awakened
Endymion sleeping on the mountain-tops.

*   *   *   *   *

Our party being once more assembled, we
wandered awhile through shady walks and overhanging woods carpeted with purple violets, and
abounding in a peculiar kind of bright blue aster,
which contrasted charmingly with the moss-grown
ground.   It was difficult to tear oneself away from
this Arcadian paradise, but on my remarking to
Jacobini what a charming place it would be during
the summer heats, he quite astonished me by say-

ing it is more than suspected of malaria, and therefore little frequented.

It was with much regret that I left Genzano and the pellucid lake, but the good Jacobini's feelings amounted almost to despair. Again he entreated us to sleep the night, but finding that impossible, contented himself by mounting into the carriage with us, and escorting us on our way. We returned by the same road as far as Ariccia, when he departed, bidding us many times *addio*, *buon viaggio*, and *rivederle*, and bearing from us solemn promises of a speedy return.

Leaving Ariccia, we mounted by an ascending road into the recesses of those great woods which clothe the Lakes of Albano and Nemi and the lower spurs of Monte Cavo. The slanting rays of the sun cast a chequered shade on the ground, covered with every blossom of the spring: violets, yellow daffodils, blue hyacinths dedicated to melancholy and the dead; the anemone, with its dark petals, sprung from the blood of Adonis; and snowdrops, called here "the tears of the Madonna." A gentle wind rustled among the lower shrubs and saplings, and mingled with the murmur of bees busy among gay patches of yellow broom. The singing of birds, particularly that of the nightingale, is never heard to such ad-

vantage as in Italian woods, where, like the *cicale*,
they seem literally to warble away their little
throats, and kill themselves with sweet songs.

The living rock here and there protruded
bare, or covered with emerald mosses and many
delicate varieties of fern plants; while overhead
waved ancient trees of chestnut, elm, and ilex,
twisted into strange shapes, like spirits writhing
in the torments of Hades. For about an hour
we wound among the mazes of this enchanting
wood, and then emerged on the summit of a hill
to another phase of all-beauteous Nature. Below
opened the Lake of Albano, unruffled, waveless,
its precipitous and wooded banks mirrored in the
calm waters. Light broke into my soul at the
sight of that beautiful lake which I had so long
looked for in vain: it came before me like the
image of a beloved and long-sought friend. Before us Monte Cavo rose in one long line from
its shores; to the left lay Castel Gondolfo, roman-
tically crowning a precipitous cliff embowered in
dark woods. The character of the scenery greatly
resembles that of the Lake of Nemi, but on a
larger scale: the same untroubled waters enclosed
in a deep cup-like basin—the same soft harmonious
beauty—the same richly-wooded mountains, rising
steeply around—the same brilliant colouring, pe-

8*

culiar to this "land of many hues"—the same
solitude, and mystic repose—the same absence of
any living being, house, or sign of life. Beautiful
as it is, there is a melancholy, plaintive look
about it, eloquently suggestive of happier times.
The shores seem heavy with sad memories of
other days. Had I not already known the Lake
of Albano to be rich in classical traditions—the
fabled land whence came the first germ of Rome
—I should have guessed from its aspect that the
past had there left its indelible imprint, and that
the history of those fair, sad shores, which even
under the joyous sun look ominous and foreboding, was to be sought in bygone centuries.

This lake lies deep in the crater of an extinct
volcano, and its waters bear that dark look peculiar to fluid spontaneously emitted by a convulsion of Nature. Few valleys or ravines break
its green sides, which descend in precipitous lines
to the margin. There is the monotony of perfect
and exquisite beauty, such as one remarks in the
classical works of Grecian sculpture, where a slight
defect or shortcoming would be almost a relief to
the over-taxed eye. An indication of rocks on
the opposite shore, slightly basaltic, marks, as
H——ns informed us, the site of Alba Longa;
for the researches of Sir William Gell have finally

settled that much-disputed question. There, as
goes the legend, once stood the palace of a
mighty king, who, in punishment for his pride,
was destroyed by fire sent from heaven by the
gods—a catastrophe supposed to have some obscure connection with the volcanic explosion to
which the lake owes its origin. The ruins of his
palace are yet pointed out in the dark bosom of
the waters, when from long drought they sink below their usual level; and the contadini tell many
fearful tales of immense grottoes, arches, and
columns; of a whirlpool in the centre, which
renders the lake dangerous for boats; and of the
spirits of the dead, which still float over the sub-
merged walls which they once inhabited.

Alba Longa, or the "White Long City," was
founded by Ascanius, the son of Æneas, who
himself was excluded, like Moses, from the
"pleasant land" promised to his followers. Æneas
dwelt on the Latin plains, near the shore on
which he had landed, on the sandy, barren spot
where the white sow had farrowed her thirty
young. After Ascanius, surnamed "Iulus," or
the "Soft-haired," who founded the city by the
calm lake which yet nurses in its bosom the ruins
of his proud palace, came Numitor and Amulius,
who divided the throne; but after a time Amulius

wickedly prevailed over his brother, and commanded his niece Sylvia, who had been born and
reared within the new city, to become a priestess
of Vesta; but Sylvia forgot her vows, and bore
the twins Romulus and Remus, who, to conceal
her shame, were borne away into the plain, and
consigned to the great river "Father Tiber,"
which divides the level land of the Campagna.
The current bore them to a wild fig tree which
grew near the site on which the Forum was afterwards built; and thus Rome came to be founded
by the twins, and Alba Longa fell into decay,
and was forgotten, until all that now remains is
that faint line of dark rock rending the green
sward.   But the Romans remembered always the
old cradle of their race, and therefore they
founded the great temple of Jupiter Latialis,
whose majestic portico once crowned the summit
of Monte Cavo, the highest point on these Alban
Hills; and there all the tribes worshipped, looking
over the broad lands of ancient Latium.

As we sat among the ilex trees many recollections inspired by the place arose. H——ns
reminded us that these wooded heights had afterwards been appropriated to the villas of Pompey
and Domitian, traces of whose summer palaces
are still distinguishable.   We followed a magni-

ficent avenue of ilex trees leading along the
upper margin of the lake into the small town of
Castel Gondolfo, where the Pope has a villa to
which he retires during the summer heats.   We
walked hurriedly through the small town—a poor
and poverty-stricken place, spite of the occasional
presence of "the Holy Father"—and descended
by a winding, tortuous path to the shore; for
H——ns was determined that we should see the
Emissary, one of the best preserved and most
striking monuments of republican Rome.   In vain
our "quiet friend" expostulated, for she by no
means fancied the climbing.   Her voice was lost
in the majority; I was for it, and so was Sculpture—three to one—so we carried the day, and
down we rapidly descended along a difficult path,
escorted by a ragged boy, who amused his leisure
time by whooping and screaming in an unintelligible *patois* to his comrades on the opposite
shore.   After a long and winding descent we
rested on the shores of the motionless lake, on an
unbroken fringe of the finest turf.

I could have wished to wander for hours on
that peaceful shore, populated by thick-coming
fancies and poetic memories; but H——ns, now
become practical as I had grown fanciful, hurried
us on, and we were fain to follow.   Vineyards

and fruit-gardens skirted the lake, the latter loaded with the delicate pink and white blossoms of the peach, the almond, and the apricot. The water's edge was strewn with stones, among which we picked up specimens of rare marbles and fragments of terra-cotta, evidences of the palaces once inhabited by Pompey and Domitian. Masses, too, of solid foundations and half-sunken walls ran into the lake terrace-wise, showing that these imperial villas, like the modern water-palaces of Como, stood literally on the water.

A large rock juts into the lake; a great tree bends down over the rock, dipping its dark branches into the waters; and a small door appears in an old wall—a suggestive door, that might lead to Hades, or Lethe, or Purgatory, or any other terrible and unreal place. The custode, a rough shepherd clothed in goats' skins, was there before us, and had opened it. We passed into an enclosed space, walled in with massive-looking Etruscan blocks of stone matted with ivy, and piled above each other as if the Titans had placed them there, and poised them without cement or mortar. This mysterious *nymphæum*, dark and cool even in the hottest day, filled with the sound of rushing waters, must have been the very trysting-place of the nymphs and sylvan deities. The spirits of the woods and the spirits of the waters, in bygone times, must have met here, and danced many a jocund measure to the sound of reedy pipes. A low arch opposite the entrance, similar in construction to that of the Cloaca Maxima, but infinitely grander and better preserved, spans a rushing, rapid current, clear as crystal, but soon lost under the dark arching recesses beyond. This was the famous Emissary of the Lake of Albano, and dates back to Rome's early history and the siege of Veii, that obstinate neighbour who for ten years disputed her sway.

After the many episodes in which my subject has tempted me to indulge, I will not particularise that well-known siege, but only recall the prophecy of the old soothsayer, who during the siege, standing on the walls of the rebellious city, declared in derision to the Romans encamped beneath, as he laughed and mocked at them, "that they might think they would take Veii, but that they never should succeed until the waters of the Lake of Alba were all spent, and flowed out into the sea no more." And when the old man was afterwards captured by stratagem, and conducted to the Roman generals, he repeated the same words; because, he said, it was the Fates who prompted him to declare what he spoke, and that, "if the waters ran out into the sea, 'woe is Rome!' but that if they be drawn off, and reach the sea no more, then it is 'woe to Veii!'" So the Romans, unable to comprehend his import, sent to consult the Oracle of Delphi, which agreed in all things with the old man's words. The Romans, therefore, who had been much molested at various times by the capricious rising of the waters within the lake, sent workmen, and bored a passage underground through the hills to the other side, where it emerged, and thus made the waters obedient for watering the lands. So the Emissary was built, and Veii fell; and this far misty legend, and ourselves, and the nineteenth century, are linked together by that low arch under which runs the rapid current into which, standing on a few rough logs of wood, we gazed!

There is a popular belief prevailing in this locality, similar to that of the Indians on the sacred Ganges, that little barks made of leaves or sticks, balanced with a lighted taper, bring the fulfilment of any special wish breathed over them in a believing spirit by those who confide them to this subterranean current—provided always that the tapers are not extinguished so long as the barks remain in sight.

I could not conceive why H———ns had so tormented the custode about bringing lights, seeing that the sun shone brightly, and had actually insisted on sending back a *messager* into the town for a bundle of *moccoletti*. Now his purpose was revealed to me, as also the motive of his active and anxious desire to conduct us to the Emissary, spite of the expostulations of our chaperon, who declared that the passage *down* "naturally suggested," as Box says to Cox, "how we *ever* should get *up!*" The little barks were soon laden—one for S. W———, another for me, and one for H———ns,—and sent sailing down the gloomy waters which flowed there centuries before Christianity descended on benighted pagans. The deep low vault and the rapid current received and bore them; and we watched their passage, and saw that the voyage promised fair, for the lights illumined the dark sides of the water-paved cavern for a long, long while, then dwindled, and at length disappeared. I wonder on what strange shore those little barks have stranded, and if the good spirits that came down to meet them will hear our prayer. H———ns was immensely anxious about his; but we each kept our own secret, and none knew the other's wish.

We left this place—the high road, as it were,

into a visionary world—and, as "Pilgrim's Progress" says, "addressed ourselves to the ascent" —a labour not easy to accomplish, seeing that the hills are as straight as a house-side, and that, by way of hastening, we chose a path where there was little or no footing. Over stones, and briers, and holes, and rocks we scrambled, sitting down now and then to rest and laugh. At length we reached the summit, breathless and hot, but merry as in the morning when we traversed the Campagna. We gave a look at the Pope's villa—an ugly, staring place, with a grand view over the lake on one hand, and the broad level expanse of sea and Campagna on the other; then seated ourselves in the carriage and wound down a rapid hill, effectually shutting out the lake and all its charms. A delightful drive through the cool evening air brought us to Rome. We saw the sun set in sheets of gold and saffron over the Mediterranean, the Campagna, and the ruins, in long streaks of glorious light. For a space the very heavens were on fire; then settled down in bars of crimson and deep blood-red. These gradually melted too, and then came pinks, and blues, and purples, reflected on the Sabine Hills, Mount Algidus, ancient Tusculum, and the ruined villas of Cicero, Adrian, and Domitian. Then night—

dark, leaden night—gradually spread her sable mantle around, and the stars came out one by one, and the moon rose, and, lighted by her pale crescent, we passed the overarching ruins by the Lateran.   What a pleasant day it had been!

CHAPTER V.

Something about Nuns and Convents—The Quirinale and Pius IX.

I HAD seen a saint made at St. Peter's when
I came first to Rome. I have now seen a nun
made, and the second ceremony edified me more
than the first, because, having deeply studied ecclesiastical Rome, I understood it better. There
is a small church on the left hand, descending
the hill from the Quattro Fontane towards Santa
Maria Maggiore, before whose door we found
ourselves at nine o'clock last Sunday morning.
Who the tutelary saint of that small church is, no
bigger than an "upper chamber," I do not know.
Our kind monk, Padre S——, who was waiting
to receive us, ushered us in, and placed us close
to the altar, which was garlanded, wreathed, and
draped with red and white and gold, mixed with
flowers and boughs. The floor of the church was
also strewed with box and bay leaves, which ex-
haled an aromatic perfume as the heavy feet of
the crowd went and came. We were early: the

altar was untenanted, a crimson desk and cushion
being placed in front for the officiating cardinal.
There was a great deal of running to and fro;
for it seemed a simple, primitive sort of place,
unused to such grand and solemn ceremonial.
The *custode* (Anglicè, "pew-opener"), a little
humpty-dumpty woman, looked all cap and ribbons, bustle and confusion. She, and the Swiss
guards in their party-coloured uniforms, standing
right and left of the altar, were incessantly at
cross-purposes, causing the poor little soul to
blush deeper and deeper at each fresh mistake.
Then there was a naughty little shred of the gar-
ment of Aaron, dressed in a surplice, who dodged
about in company with another little priestikin,
and caused great scandal by the faces they made
from behind the altar at each other—an *incon-
venance* instantly and sternly checked by a tall
and solemn priest, who, laying violent hands on
both, drove them ignominiously forth among the
crowd. It was a festa—a great festa—and they
wanted to enjoy it their own way: the poor things
knew no better.

After the pew-opener had rushed about in and
out of the crowd many times, putting chairs in
impossible places, where they wouldn't stand, and
displaying various evidences of a temporary aber-

ration of intellect, a bell sounded lustily—a buzz and hush went round the crowd — the guards opened a passage—and Cardinal M——, a venerable man entirely clothed in red, advanced and knelt on the cushion prepared for him. He was followed by a suite of gentlemen habited in black, somewhat in the Sir Walter Raleigh style, wearing swords and chains, who, during his orisons, stood around him. After he had risen and taken his place in front of the altar opposite the congregation, two ladies, the Countess M—— and Mrs. S——, wearing veils, advanced, accompanied by priests, and leading by the hand two little children. They took their places on chairs facing the altar. After a pause, and some singing of female voices from behind the altar, four sisters advanced, who, having previously taken the lesser vows, were now to make what is called their profession. They were habited as Sisters of Mercy, wearing black robes, and white linen cloths folded over and about their heads in those indescribable coifs peculiar to nuns. Each bore a lighted candle in her hand. Their eyes were bent on the ground, and they were accompanied by two other elderly sisters, similarly habited, who had already taken the full vows. This solemn procession passed into the enclosure around the altar, each sister

making her reverence to the benevolent-looking
cardinal seated on his fald-stool, the rear being
brought up by two lovely children, fair and pure
as alabaster, habited as little angels, with draperies of blue over tunics of pale pink, sandals on
their feet, and wings covered with feathers on
their shoulders. These little creatures bore each
a salver; one containing wreaths of the brightest
and freshest flowers, the other crowns of green
thorns, their great dagger-points standing out
several inches—thorns that recall those encircling
the head of the divine "Man of Sorrow," so
pathetically rendered by Guido and Carlo Dolce.

By the time these various groups had ranged
themselves around the altar, the sacred space was
quite full. It was a rich and varied tableau; the
calm, venerable cardinal in the centre; on one
side the six nuns, in their dark habits, bearing,
as the wise virgins of old, "their lights burning;"
on the other, the group of attendant gentlemen
and priests; the little angels in their gay draperies; the veiled ladies and their little charges;
with the great crimson velvet curtains framing all
in heavy folds. Music now burst forth from a
hidden choir in joyous strains befitting the happy
celebration of the celestial espousals. The cardinal was invested with splendid robes of white

and gold, and a jewelled mitre was placed on his head. The ladies (secular) then advanced, and, kneeling at his feet, presented the two children, who received at his hands the consecrated oil on their foreheads—a renewal of the baptismal vows, answering to our own ceremony of confirmation. Oil that has been solemnly blessed can only be used in the most solemn rites, such as the coronation of sovereigns, the administration of extreme unction, and other exceptional occasions; and is only to be touched by the hands of a priest. A fillet of white silk was then fastened round the heads of the children, which gave them the appearance of early Christian catechumens. At the conclusion of this graceful preface to the other ceremony, the children, and the two ladies who acted as their sponsors, retired to their seats, and were seen no more.

Music broke the pauses, joyous Hallelujahs and Te Deums and Jubilates; amid which songs of praise, the nuns, advancing, kissed the hand of the cardinal. Their confessor, a tall ill-favoured man, who had entered with them and taken his place by the altar, now rose, and in Italian besought the cardinal to permit him to address a few words of exhortation to his spiritual daughters.

Such an occasion would furnish an admirable

opportunity for a man of eloquence and intellect to make a splendid discourse, but the *padre* here present was a common, coarse creature, who brawled in a high-pitched voice, like a Presbyterian minister, for about twenty minutes, in praise of virginity and of the sacrifice these *coraggiose giovani*, as he styled them, were about to make, and then sat down. The nuns again advanced opposite to the cardinal, and knelt; the little angels, who already looked very faint and weary, drew near; and the ceremony proceeded.

I cannot attempt to give all the particulars of this long and complicated service. I notice the salient points only. One nun, representing her fellows—all of whom bore lighted candles of a size much resembling a torch—made a speech in Italian to the cardinal, to the effect that she and her fellows desired to lay aside all worldly pomp, desires, and vanities, and to attach themselves wholly to that Divine Bridegroom who will one day descend to claim his own. They desired to suffer, to obey, to renounce all and everything, for his sake—father and mother and friends—so as to be found of Him. This was all pronounced in a clear, cheerful voice, without any apparent emotion whatever; in fact, it wanted modulation to make it interesting; and great and noble as was

9*

the sacrifice they were making, it lacked that poetic charm of melancholy and regret with which the imagination invests a nun's vows, separating her from all she loves in the *visible* world, for the sake and love of that *invisible* country—"that bourne from which no traveller returns"—beyond the skies.

At the close of the nun's oration the cardinal addressed certain questions to them all, and I heard them promise "to go wherever they were sent." What a world lay in these simple words —the renunciation of what we love next to life, our liberty—"to go whither they were sent." Poor souls! what a vow, and what fortitude would be required to fulfil it, when we remember that these, being Sisters of Mercy, would be employed in nursing the sick! "To go whither they are sent," into contagion, filth, sorrow, and death—to minister to the wants of the suffering wretch that the world disowns—to receive his last sigh—to close his starting eyes! Oh, holy and sacred vocation, when sincerely fulfilled!

The cardinal then took a large pair of scissors from off the altar, and cut from the head of each a handful of hair, which he presented to them. Receiving the hair from him, they cast it from them with these words, pronounced in clear, round, unhesitating accents: *"Rinunzio al mondo e a tutte le sue vanità."*   There was almost *hate* and *defiance* in the tone and the action, as though the thought of this world was sin, and pain, and sorrow; but no one present could for a moment question its entire sincerity—it was the free, spontaneous expression of the internal essence.   The cardinal then addressed them in Italian.

"Mie sorelle," said he, "you have chosen, like Mary, the 'better part;' you will be the brides of that unseen and eternal Bridegroom whose coming the Church militant earnestly awaits.   Will you, like Him, choose the crown of thorns, or will you prefer the chaplet of flowers?   Here are both.   I desire that you make your choice."

The little angels now advanced, bearing each their salver.

"Eminentissimo," replied the nun who had all along acted as spokeswoman, "we only wish in all things to follow the example of our Divine Lord; we beseech the blessed Virgin, *Maria Santissima*, and all the saints to help us in this our resolve.   Like Jesus, we desire to wear the crown of thorns, which we now take."

Each advanced, and taking a crown of thorns from off the salver, two elder sisters fixed it on the top of their white coifs.   Bearing these marks

of our Saviour's agony, they had accomplished the
symbolic rites of the Church, and had become
eternally dedicated to Him in time as in eternity.
They kissed the hand of the cardinal, then tenderly
saluted each other; and, after listening to some
more joyous music from the invisible choir in
celebration of the mystic espousals, they withdrew
as they had come. I could see them well as they
passed out. Some were strikingly handsome, young,
with grand massive features, and deep, dark,
glancing eyes, only to be seen in the South—
profound, fathomless, glorious, as the depths of
their own blue heavens! Peace go with the holy
maids, and joy in the great vineyard of the Lord,
whither they were bound; and may they never
repent those solemn oaths, chronicled by the Church
in our hearing!

"*Ahi, poverine!*" exclaimed that excellent creature, Padre S——, when all was over. "*Dio li
protegge!* What a life—what sacrifices! *Ah, chi
lo sa!*" And his honest eyes ran over with tears,
for he—a monk of Valombrosa—*knew* what it was
to take up that Cross here below, and wreathe it
with flowers of humility and resignation, when it
is most heavy and most bitter.

The church of San Antonio, on the Esquiline,
is known to every one as the place where the

animals are blessed. It is also well known to
Romans as the convent where are manufactured
the palms used by the Pope and cardinals in the
high mass at St. Peter's on Palm Sunday. This
year no less than twelve hundred were woven out
of the *canne*, or reeds (growing in waving forests
on the banks of rivers and in marshy places), by
the industrious nuns, who, living under what is
called *clausura*, can never leave their monastery
like the free, but certainly more heroic, "Sisters
of Mercy."

Padre S—— took us to see the great palm
made for the Pope, and sent to him every year
from San Antonio. He, poor man, was in ecstasy
over its elegance and fancy. If it had been a rare
cinque-cento toy worked by the hand of the immortal Cellini, he could not have more extolled
it. It certainly was wonderful how the conceits
and fancies of grapes, and wheat-ears, and leaves,
and flowers, could all be cut out of hard round
reeds; but the design was poor and confused, and
the introduction of artificial flowers into the festoons
gave the whole a tawdry appearance. It was a
huge thing, nearly six feet high.

But what engaged me much more than the
palm was a sight we saw in the interior of the
cloister, whither, thanks to our tonsured friend

(who is the confessor of these good sisters), we
had penetrated. There was a small table immediately below a heavy double-iron grating, shaped
like a window in the wall. At this table sat an
elderly man of the working class and a boy. Behind the grating, and distinctly visible, was a real
"cloistered nun," conversing with these her relatives, and all the while busily plying her fingers
in weaving, and cutting, and twisting a palm for
the coming festa. Her figure and head were wrapped
in a mantle of black serge; her face was enclosed
in a close-setting coif. She was young and positively beautiful. Fresh roses mantled in her cheeks,
and her eyes quite pierced the envious bars. She
looked gay, smiling, and happy, and was conversing on evidently cheerful and animating subjects in a low voice with her relatives. I could
scarcely take my eyes from her—she seemed positively to irradiate the gloomy precincts around
her. Padre S—— informed me that nuns are at
all times permitted thus to meet and freely con-
verse with friends and relatives.

"But," said I, "should they *abuse* the indul-
gence, what then?"

"Oh!" said he, "that rarely occurs; but in
such a case the abbess would interfere and ad-

monish the sister. Would you like to see the mother-superior?"

"Oh, extremely!"

"Well, you shall see her; for she is *una buonis-sima creatura e molto mia amica.*"

So we passed into an inner room, and sat down before precisely such another little table, under just such a double grating. As Padre S—— passed the lovely nun, she respectfully rose and saluted him. This attention was shown by virtue of his office of confessor to the community. After waiting some time, a little old wrinkled woman, bent nearly double by age, emerged from the dark recesses beyond, like some fairy of the good old days. Her countenance, though extremely aged, expressed mildness and amiability. She saluted us kindly, and seemed quite delighted at our praises of the Pope's great palm.

"*Si,*" replied she, "*un bel lavoro molto bravo.*"

We had not many subjects in common, especially as the good old lady declined to consider us *Christians;* but we got on very tolerably notwithstanding. She looked at our children and asked their ages, and admired them—until, quite ashamed of martyrising her any longer, I begged to *levarle l'incomodo* (as the Romans say), and

withdrew.   Certainly my impression of the nuns
of San Antonio is that they are cheerful, happy,
and in the enjoyment of all becoming freedom.

Many of the boasted hills of Rome exist but
in name, or in the excited imaginations of antiquarians; but the Quirinale is really a respectable
and visible eminence, conspicuous from all quarters
of the city. Baths and temples decorated its base.
A temple to the Fidius Dius (or of good faith) is
particularly mentioned—a deity with a horn—with
whom, assuredly, the Romans had very small
dealings.   On the summit, near the site of the
very magnificent but small church of St. Andrew,
belonging to the Jesuits, rose the stately temple
of Quirinus, dedicated to Romulus.   When that
unprincipled, though fortunate, founder of young
Rome had established his brigand dominion over
a motley collection of exiles, refugees, thieves,
and murderers, gathered by promises of refuge,
and certainty of warlike spoils from all parts of
Italy, he suddenly, after a long and prosperous
reign, disappeared from the presence of the multitude during an assembly of the people without
the city. The heavens darkened, clouds gathered
over his throne, a blackness as of night obscured
the day, and thunder and loud winds burst forth,
as if announcing some tremendous convulsion of

Nature. When the tempest passed and the light reappeared, Romulus was gone.

The people declared that he had been murdered, but the priests and patricians maintained that he was caught up to heaven, and that it behoved the quirites and plebs to worship him as a god. The question was satisfactorily settled by the credulity or ingenuity of a certain Alban, Julius Proculus by name, descended from Ascanius, the founder of the "Long White City," who affirmed that on his way to the Forum, Romulus had met him, ennobled and dazzling in countenance, and arrayed in radiant armour. Julius, astonished at the apparition, thus addressed it: "For what misbehaviour of ours, O king! or by what accident have you so untimely left us in utter calamity, and sunk the whole city in inexpressible sorrow?" To which the shade graciously replied, "It pleased the gods, my good Proculus, that for awhile I should dwell with men and found a great and glorious city, and afterwards return to the heavens from whence I came. Farewell. Go tell the Romans that by the exercise of temperance and fortitude they shall attain the highest pitch of human greatness, and I, the god Quirinus, will ever be propitious to them."

Thus spoke the unrighteous murderer of his

brother, and disappeared. So a temple was built, and the royal impostor Romulus was deified and honoured under the name of *Quirites*, as a martial or warrior god; and the hill was called Quirinus on which his temple stood, and is so named even to this day.

On the summit of the height appears the magnificent fountain of Monte Cavallo, so named from the horses and their god-like leaders, Castor and Pollux. The names of Phidias and Praxiteles are engraven on the pedestals, and antiquarians agree that they are of Grecian workmanship. Their exquisite classical beauty is, at all events, beyond dispute. Between them rises an obelisk of red granite, brought from the mausoleum of Augustus, where it had been placed to commemorate some Egyptian triumph of Rome's first emperor. That obelisk, bathed in the sunlight, carries back one's mind to the burning sand-deserts bordering the Nile, and to gigantic temples and mysterious rites of which Herodotus himself could not write without trembling. Now its base is bathed by a pure and delicious fountain. Beyond are churches and edifices bordering the ample piazza. In one corner we catch a glimpse of the Rospigliosi Palace, embowered in trees; opposite rise the walls of the Colonna Gardens,

overmantling with verdure and |loading the air
with the perfume of roses and orange groves,
under whose shade the Papal cavalry are wont to
meet, groom their horses, sing martial songs, and
swear "in very choice Italian" as unconcernedly
as if the ground they stood on was not consecrated by world-wide legends of the classic
past.

On the opposite side, facing the fountain,
extends the vast palace of the Quirinale,* crowning the hill like a diadem, and descending through
whole streets in its interminable length. It im-
presses the imagination from the very simplicity
of its architecture, so essentially different from
the florid magnificence prevailing at the Vatican.
It was at the Quirinale, built by Paul III. and
Gregory XIII., that the conclaves of the Sacred
College always assembled; and at that window
which one sees conspicuous over the grand entrance the new Pope was presented to the Roman
people. A place renowned as the scene where
the ancient Romans worshipped the temporal
power of their deified king, and the Catholic
world for ages received its chief, must demand
from me some few details.

When the Pope is dead, the cardinal-chamber-

---

* Now the palace of the King of United Italy.

lain knocks three times at the door of his chamber,
calling on him by his Christian and family name,
and his title as Pope. After a pause he turns to
the attendant clergy and notaries, saying, "*Dunque
è morto.*" The fisherman's ring is taken from his
finger and broken in pieces; the great bell of the
Capitol tolls, and the bells of every one of the innumerable churches in Rome respond to its deep
and solemn note. The Sacred College of Cardinals meanwhile assembles, whilst the body of the
deceased pontiff is exposed to the sight of the
people who come and kiss his feet.

On the ninth day the cardinals meet in the
Quirinale chapel, where the psalm, "Veni, Crea-
tor," is sung. The immense extent of the palace
on this side, running down the Via Pia to the
Quattro Fontane, is entirely divided into little
suites of chambers, inhabited only on these
solemn occasions, when, in order to prevent any
possibility of communication from without during
the sitting of the conclave, the cardinals are confined there until after the election of a new pope.
Each room contains a bed, a few chairs, and a
table. The cardinal princes once installed in these
dismal little cells, which are hung with green
serge, the doors of the palace are walled up, as
are also the windows, except one pane, just suf-

ficient to admit a gloomy light into the conclave.

The Prince of Savelli, by virtue of an hereditary privilege, keeps the gates, and provisions
are conveyed to the cardinals and their attendants
by means of revolving circular cupboards, such as
one sees used in convents. There are confessors,
doctors, surgeons, two barbers, and a carpenter,
also shut up. The cardinals rise at six o'clock,
when a bell rings, and a voice is heard in the
long corridors calling out, "Ad capellam Do-
mini."

The election, which takes place in the chapel,
is by ballot; the great powers of Catholic Europe
having each the power of a single veto against
any single cardinal, but no more. When the
number of votes makes it evident who will be
elected, a bell sounds, and the name of the
chosen cardinal is pronounced aloud. He is then
asked if he accepts the election, on responding to
which demand in the affirmative (for history in-
forms us of no pontiff who ever refused the
proffered honour), the cardinals fall back respectfully, leaving him alone. He then announces by
what appellation he intends to reign, it having
been the custom for the popes to change their
names at their election ever since the time of

Sergius IV., who, being christened *Peter*, declined
to bear the name given by Christ to the first
among the Apostles. The new Pope is then
arrayed in white and crimson, red embroidered
shoes bearing the cross are put on his feet, the
cardinals kiss the cross, and he is invested with
the fisherman's ring.

The "Ecce Sacerdos Magnus" is then sung
by the fine Papal choir, unaccompanied by in-
strumental music, and the cardinal-deacon, preceded by a mason, a carpenter, and the master
of the ceremonies, proceeds to the window in the
Loggia over the grand entrance to announce to
the people the election of the Pope.

An immense multitude fills the piazza. The
windows, the roofs, are one moving mass of human
beings, ebbing and flowing like the stormy waves
of an angry sea. All Rome is there, the plebeian
and the patrician, brought together by one common sentiment of intense curiosity. Cries and
screams announce the excitable nature of the fiery
Italians. They can brook no delay—the cardinal
is too long in coming—the carpenter is a *birbante*,
and they curse the mason, and send him to the
infernal gods of both ancient and modern Erebus
for his laziness. "*Ci vuol il nostro Papa. Facci
vedere il nostro Papa!*" "We must see him! Give

us our Pope!" thunders on all sides. The smaller
canaille mount sacrilegiously on the beauteous
statues of Castor and Pollux, bestride the Grecian
steeds without ceremony, and fling around the
water from the basin on the crowd who cannot
escape, crying out to be shown their Pope. The
guards, in this moment of interregnum, are of no
avail; they are mocked at and disregarded. They,
too, end by joining in the cry of "*Il Papa—il
nuovo Papa!*" It is a moment of thrilling interest,
of dramatic suspense. Suddenly there is a great
pause. A silence, a stillness as of death, falls on
that assembled multitude. The wall of brick
that built up the window totters, falls with a crash,
the cardinal-deacon stands forth on the Loggia,
and the soft music of the choir is heard in the
distance. At the sight of the cardinal there is a
hush. The crowd trembles, rushes forward, and
then again is still. A religious silence reigns.

"I announce to you," says his Eminence,
"joyful tidings; the Most Eminent and Reverend
Cardinal N——, having taken the name of ——,
is elected Pope."

The piazza resounds with enthusiastic roars,
shouts, and cries of delight and triumph; the
silver trumpets sound clear and pure above the
riot; the great guns of Castel San Angelo bang

forth their iron bolts; and every fort in Rome
unites in chorus with the deep harmonious sound
of the great bell of St. Peter's, and the bells of
every other church in the city.

In the midst of this exulting jubilee, when
earth calls on the mighty echoes of the mountains and the high vault of heaven to respond to
and participate in its joy, the father of the Catholic world himself appears on the balcony, and in-
dulges the enthusiasm of a delirious people by his
presence. When Pius IX. was elected, his tender
heart was so overcome by these overwhelming
greetings, that he actually burst into a flood of
tears, and was removed fainting from the Loggia.
But the people have not yet done. After the
Pope withdraws, they rush forward, and, by virtue
of an ancient privilege, proceed to the interior of
the palace where the conclave sat, seize on everything they can find as their lawful booty, until the
illumination of the city calls off the uproarious
rabble to a wider arena wherein to *sfogare* their
boiling passions.

It was from this historic window that Pius IX.
was in the habit of showing himself to the enthusiastic Romans at the period of his wild popularity, when they called him forth to heap
blessings on his head, to applaud and cheer him

for the boon of liberty his government insured
them. Here he received all the ovations which
an excited and grateful nation are capable of
rendering. Sometimes he was called forth in rain
and wind, and came, obedient to their wishes, to
gratify them by his presence, and dispense blessings around—blessings of price, coming from a
good and a Christian man who lives near his
God. Those two short years saw many thrilling
scenes of love, devotion, and enthusiasm, many
gorgeous pageants, many soul-inspiring services,
when the temporal and spiritual powers invested
in the beloved Pope seemed to render him more
than mortal in the eyes of his people. But the
dark days came; the chord was too tightly drawn
—it needs must slacken. The excellent and
saintly man, in his simple-hearted goodness,
granted weighty reforms too rapidly and readily.
The excited people, finding they had but to ask,
grew senseless and unreasonable, and desired that
Pius should head a red republic—a moral chaos.
The fickle population, accustomed to action and
excitement, could brook no repose—pageants and
sights must amuse them, laws be destroyed, and
new concessions keep their minds on fire. The
Pope, unconscious of the gulf opening beneath
him, confident in his people's affection and his

10*

own justice and rectitude, for a time headed the
course of events, flung himself in the rushing tide
of the changing time, and endeavoured to please
every party by his compliance. But it would not
do; he could not conscientiously, and he would
not wrongfully, answer the expectations of a
licentious and now brutalised populace. He would
have secured their freedom, but they yelled for
anarchy. The wild flames of revolution of the
tremendous '48 were abroad, and soon reached
the walls of the ancient queen of cities.

The people, finding that, *reformer* though he
was, Pius would never become a *revolutionist*,
came to hate their idol, and sought to tear him
down from the household altars which they had
reared to him. Then came the senseless and
cruel murder of Count Rossi at the Palazzo della
Cancellería—that patriotic and enlightened minister
who was the temporal support of the Papal throne.
Then came rumours of war and danger and rebellion. The same people who had once so
loved him, now gazed at the Pope in stern and
ominous silence. Then came the attack on the
Quirinale, where he lived—the brutal attack on
the sovereign who would have spent himself for
the people God had placed him to rule over.
Then he was no longer safe in once happy Rome;

for a republic was to be established, and, save the Swiss guard—faithful as steel—he was alone and undefended. Then came the flight. Then he passed out of the great portal (where first he had been saluted by the unstable Romans) disguised as a priest, and accompanied by the Bavarian ambassador—Count Spaur—and fled over the frontiers to Mola di Gaeta, where he was received by the King of Naples, and lived many long months in a kind of splendid captivity.

Another pope, years ago, was dragged from the Quirinale, which would seem fatal to the Papal power, by a different, though not less brutal, act of violence, when General Radet, the envoy of Napoleon, scaled the garden walls at the head of a band of soldiers, and at three o'clock in the morning forced his way into the sleeping-room of the venerable Pius VII. They obliged him to rise, dress, and accompany them, with his faithful minister, Cardinal Pacca, to a carriage in waiting, and thus in the silence of the night bore off the Pope a prisoner. After driving some time towards Florence, the Pope asked Cardinal Pacca if he had brought with him any money. Your Holiness knows," said he, "I was dragged out of my apartment as you were from yours, and had no opportunity of taking anything." On search-

ing their purses they found nothing but a few
bajocchi (pence). "See," exclaimed Pius VII.,
"all that remains to me of my kingdom!"

I have been led to greater length than I had
intended in recounting the vicissitudes recalled by
the Quirinale; and I must now relate my own im-
pressions when I yesterday visited that interesting
palace. I entered by the portal under that same
historic window in the front of the palace. An
enormous *cortile* occupies the centre of the building, surrounded by a fine arcade, from which
grand marble staircases ascend. This *cortile* was
as public as the streets when the Pope inhabited
the palace; and although the party-coloured Swiss
guard used ostentatiously to parade up and down,
bearing their halberds, all the dirty little boys of
the quarter found a convenient play-ground in
the cool shade of the pillared corridors. The
bocchi balls rolled; and that everlasting game with
their fingers, "*Uno, due, tre*," which the Italians
do really seem to understand from the very hour
of their birth, proceeded unmolested. Now and
then, when a cardinal or a monsignore appeared,
they would stare, stand aside, and then begin
again, nothing abashed.

On mounting a fine staircase, we entered a
nobly-proportioned hall richly decorated with

frescoes, from whence opens the chapel where
the conclave for the election of the popes is
held, and where the dove is said to descend
on the head of the elected cardinal.   These
mysterious precincts, however, are not visible
to strangers.   Three ante-rooms lined with
beautiful marbles are next passed, ending in a
kind of corridor lighted by a spacious window
looking out to the front of the palace.   This
is the window so celebrated in Papal history
as the scene of such varied events, and which,
during the sitting of the conclave, is walled up.
Beyond is a splendid apartment lined with fine
Gobelin tapestry representing subjects from our
Saviour's life, and opening into a still grander
hall, furnished in a similar manner, but more resplendent with gold and coloured marbles, where,
under a canopy of crimson velvet, the popes gave
audience to crowned heads and magnates of the
highest rank.   The chairs are of wood, and without cushions, as no one, of whatever rank, is permitted a more comfortable seat while in the presence of his Holiness, who is, however, himself
accommodated with a most luxurious *poltrona*
(literally an idle-chair).   Conspicuous in every
room are placed one if not two superbly-carved
crucifixes of gold, ebony, ivory, and precious

gems—striking mementoes in these gilded saloons. Next in order comes another audience-room of smaller dimensions, but still superb; and so on and on to a snug little boudoir, or writing-room, where the Pope's arm-chair is still prepared under a velvet canopy, before a table on which stands a large crucifix. Shelves surround the room, curtained with crimson silk; that colour also prevailing in the Pope's bedroom—a nice quiet little room, where the Vicar of Christ upon earth lays him down to rest on a small brass bedstead, screened with curtains of red silk. Two or three diminutive chests of drawers, a sofa, and a few chairs constitute all the furniture. A *bénitier* for holy water hangs against the wall. A *prie-dieu* desk for private devotion, and some crucifixes and religious ornaments, complete the arrangements of the room. It may not be generally known that Pius began life as a soldier, and belonged for many years to the Guardia Nobile, whose especial province it is to guard the person of the pontiff, whom they never quit day or night, but sleep outside the door of his chamber. The late Pope, Gregory, perceiving his vocation for a religious life, advised Pius to renounce the military career, which he accordingly did, and was ordained a priest, taking part soon after in a missionary ex-

pedition to South America.   Perhaps few modern
popes have known so much of real practical work
as Pius.   I have before mentioned the charming
and benignant expression of his countenance.   His
features are good, and although beaming with
unmistakable kindness, convey nothing vulgar or
trivial.   It is a fine, solid-looking head, with grey
hair cut à *la* Titus.   In his busts, otherwise re-
markably like him, one misses the placid and
affectionate expression of his black eyes, which
diffuse a calm peacefulness that must be felt even
by those most inclined to dispute his influence.
In manner he is kind, though quiet and reserved.
He rises at half-past six in the morning, and,
which is extraordinary in an Italian, shaves himself; for he dislikes unnecessary attendance.   His
toilet over, he says mass alone in his private
chapel, and hears another in public afterwards.
This is to Pius the most solemn and important
act of his life.   At half-past eight he has fulfilled
his pontifical duties and fortified his soul by
prayer and communion.   His mind is now free
and disengaged for the labours of the day.   A
light breakfast of coffee and a few biscuits follows,
according to the Italian fashion, and then begin
his various avocations—Maestri di Camera, Camerieri Segreti, ministers of state, cardinals, prefects,

and ambassadors now crowd the ante-chambers, and are received by him without distinction.

In many of the saloons there are good pictures, principally of the Decadence; but I was particularly struck by the principal chapel, painted entirely in fresco by Guido and Albano. It is quite a little *bijou*—so fresh and glowing, one might fancy the colours but of yesterday. A large altar-piece of the Annunciation is, to my thinking, one of the most perfect and exquisite works of Guido, although Rome boasts such matchless and numerous specimens of his skill.

After passing these suites of rooms we reached the Pope's dining-room—a quiet, unadorned apartment, where he eats alone under the eternal *baldacchino*, with a crucifix placed opposite. Ever since the too worldly repasts of Leo X. it has been etiquette for the popes to dine alone, in the most simple and frugal manner. It is the highest honour for reigning sovereigns to be admitted to the Papal table, and one rarely accorded. At Castello, or elsewhere, during the *villeggiatura*, when etiquette is somewhat relaxed, a few cardinals and prelates are sometimes, but rarely, invited. Pius's dinner is said to cost only one *scudo* (about five shillings), and to be discussed in twenty minutes, during which short time he converses with the secretary

of state.   After dinner, like a true Italian, he
retires to his room and takes a short siesta. Then
he drives out, and when without the walls alights
to walk on the public road.

The windows of the Quirinale overlook delicious gardens which slope down the steep sides
of Monte Cavello, and are divided into stately
terraces by high clipped hedges of yew and evergreen oak, bordered by statues and Termini.
Bright fountains, *jets d'eau,* and parterres of flowers
enliven the centre of each division.   Under these
dark cypress groves and ilex trees a perpetual
coolness reigns; massive sculptured balustrades
edge the hill, and long flights of marble steps
descend to sequestered shrubberies below, whence
winding paths conduct to cascades gushing from
rocky banks—an elegant, though somewhat gloomy,
plaisance, well adapted to the tonsured grandees
for whose enjoyment it was designed.

.

CHAPTER VI.

THE ceremonies of the Holy Week occupy
every day, and every night too, I verily believe,
during the entire week.   How the priests live
through it all, working and fasting, is an enigma;
but they manage to survive, and come out at
Easter as rosy and plump as ever.   The Sistine
Chapel, where the "Tenebræ" and "Miserere"
are performed on the two days preceding Good
Friday, is besieged by thousands of infatuated
females for hours before the services begin, all
struggling to obtain a front position on the forms
placed behind the screen in the lower half of the
chapel, which (as this, the private oratory of the
Pope, is supposed to be inaccessible to women)
are pushed back as far as possible.

I, for my part, took the whole affair with great
composure, and walked quietly up the Sala Regia
about four o'clock.   The ascent was beset with

Swiss guards, their brilliant uniforms and glancing steel accoutrements looking exceedingly picturesque and mediæval; hundreds of ladies in black, gentlemen in evening dress, and militia and military heroes in full uniform trooped up this truly magnificent and regal entrance to the countless splendours of the Vatican, all laughing, talking, and joking with quite praiseworthy forgetfulness of the solemn nature of the anniversary. Some ladies tried to smuggle in camp-stools under their petticoats—a *ruse* instantly detected and ruthlessly exposed by the all-seeing officials; while others, coming in greater numbers than their tickets allowed, were remorselessly sent back, spite of lamentations and reproaches in unmistakably Anglican-Italian.

It was a scene of confusion, irreverence, and frivolity; men pushing onwards, and recklessly separating groups of terrified ladies; guards pouncing on delinquents; and bold mammas dragging their staring daughters past quiet foreigners—Catholics, of course—who looked round all aghast at their irreverent haste and thoroughly English rudeness.

Arrived at the Sala Regia—at the summit of the stairs from whence both the Sistine and Pauline Chapels open — the scene grew ten times wilder. That lofty hall, so nobly proportioned, the walls glittering with frescoes and gilding, and adorned with clustered branches of magnificent candelabra—where on ordinary occasions unbroken silence reigns, and the very odour of sanctity floats around—a spot of reverent waiting and awful expectation, whether to the Catholic about to visit the shrine sanctified by the constant presence of Christ's vicar, or to the artistic devotee viewing for the first time the immortal works of Michel Angelo and his predecessors—that majestic and suggestive hall which, as I write, rises before me in all its pomp, shaded by a chastened light, half concealing, half displaying the great frescoes and the mysterious doors, some veiled by falling curtains, others opening into endless corridors and galleries, is now, alas! desecrated into a street thoroughfare!

Thousands of men and women, gathered from the four quarters of the globe, are rushing about, crowding every space, treading on each other's heels, talking, wondering, pushing; every face turned towards the open door, with its ample drapery of crimson, leading into the Sistine Chapel, which they are all firmly resolved to enter at all risks. And though that door is guarded by military—obstinate Swiss guards, who, if Venus herself fresh from Olympus, or all the Circes and Armidas that ever existed in fact or fable, tried to cajole, would not budge one single inch—still, so vast is the crowd, its own weight carrying it irresistibly onward, that all slowly disappear under the overhanging curtain.

Every one knows that the Sistine Chapel is not large. Imagine, then, what it must be when, in the space assigned to the public—in which five hundred might commodiously sit—ten thousand persons are, by some miracle of crushing, collected. Imagine the heat, the squeezing, the elbows poked into one's sides, the furious glances, the hatred, malice, and uncharitableness of all those living beings, each wanting to see and to hear; and all, save a few in the front, effectually prevented from doing either, and furiously incensed in consequence. I doubt if the pagan audience collected in the Flavian Amphitheatre to see men torn by wild beasts could be more savage. For myself, I, symbolically speaking, gave up the ghost in terror and dismay, but by good luck getting pushed against the side of the ladies' box, I carefully kept my place, and tried to collect my senses. This box, or enclosure, was as full as stuffing could make it, and the heat excessive. At the entrance, one of the Papal camerieri, dressed in doublet, hose, and high Elizabethan ruff, kept up a show of order. Still more ladies would keep crowding in, despite his remonstrances.

"*Le prego, le supplico, signora; di non montare, non c' è posto, è pieno.*"

"*Mais,*" says some English mamma with two lean daughters, "*vous pouvez faire un po di place je suis sûre pour questa signora,*" pushing forward first one, then the other daughter.

"*No, madama,*" replies the cameriere angrily; "*impossibile.*"

"*Mais, moussu,*" says a fat old lady, who has been perseveringly elbowing her way upwards, and has, spite of all opposition, firmly planted her foot on the prohibited steps, "*je vois une place— un posto, là, là*—let me go!" And she makes a dash forwards.

"*No, signora,*" again replies the cameriere, placing his arm across the opening, which the belligerent lady disregarding, pushes madly aside; and a struggle—yes, actually a struggle begins, ending in the signal defeat and consequent retreat of the fat lady, who is violently landed on the ground, looking extremely red and furious; the cameriere, excited and scarlet also, exclaiming in a low voice, "*Ma, corpo di Bacco!* must I then call in the *carabinieri* against these *Inglesi?*"

Neither the Pope nor the cardinals were visible. The Gregorian chant, in which the Psalms are sung, had begun, and the lights, fixed on a triangular stand near the altar, were burning. This stand, typical of the Trinity, holds fifteen lights, one of which is extinguished at the conclusion of each psalm. This usage is explained by some as symbolising the prophets, who were persecuted and successively put to death before the coming of the Saviour; others represent it as signifying the abandonment and desertion He suffered from all his disciples in his last hours. The last light is not extinguished, but withdrawn behind the altar, in allusion to the Saviour's entombment and subsequent resurrection; the "Tenebræ" being an office of mourning commemorating the death of the Redeemer, while its triple celebration is in allusion to the three days during which his body remained in the tomb. The music is entirely vocal, and intensely monotonous; for, by some unexplained etiquette, the organ is never heard in the presence of the Holy Father. No pomp, no gorgeous spectacle can compensate for the absence of that thrilling, overwhelming burst that carries the soul upwards in a rushing torrent of delicious harmony. St. Cecilia is said to have invented the

organ in a moment of ecstatic inspiration. It is
a pretty legend, and fitly symbolises the heavenly
influence of that noble instrument. But to return.
Suffocated, cramped, and confused, it seemed to
me the Psalms would never end. Impatience became general, and everybody around was perpetually popping up and down to see how many
lights remained. "Now there's only two left," I
heard. "Now there is only one!" As the moment approached for the commencement of the
"Miserere," the excitement increased tenfold.
Fresh crowds pushed in through the door, determined, *coûte que coûte*, to storm the barriers of
half-fainting women. Some retreated; some were
borne out insensible, the guards coming to their
rescue; others firmly stood their ground. Again
the fight began with the old ladies and the cham-
berlain, and again he victoriously repulsed their
assault. All the lights had disappeared; evening
was darkening into night; the chapel lay wrapped
in a dim, subdued twilight, the audience massed
into grey and black shadows; the glorious roof,
painted by Michel Angelo, became indistinct and
misty. . . . . . It was an hour of solemn commun-
ing and awful contemplation, met, as we seemed,
on the threshold of the tomb to celebrate the
cruel abandonment of the Divine One, surrounded

by typical darkness and lamentations, prefiguring
the agony of his soul, when the bitter cry was
wrung from Him, "My God, my God, why hast
thou forsaken me!"

After a brief pause the first long-drawn notes
of the "Miserere" echoed through the gloom—
soft, unearthly, spiritual—sounds as of celestial
souls suffering the torments of the damned, and
calling on heaven and earth to listen while they
breathed forth their agony.   Now a high note
struck on the ear, thrilling in its acuteness—a
note suggestive of corporeal suffering from an incorporeal being.   As it died away, other voices
took up the wailing strain, breaking off like the
first in vague, melancholy sighs.   Then came a
convulsive thrill, a quivering shake in the sad
minor key in which the whole is sung, followed
by a few notes of delicious cadence, rich and
flowing, as if a glimpse of heaven—an angel visit
—had for a moment broken the spell of torture.
Brief respite!   Again sounds the same piercing
cry, and again it floats away into unutterable voiceless chaos.   As the sad strains swelled in tearful
modulations, the shadows deepened, and night
came to shroud, as it were, and bear them in her
sable bosom to the realms above, where angels
wept as they listened, and all the glory of heaven

11*

grew dim at the remembrance of the Saviour's
agonies.

Still, spite of the touching and profoundly
devotional character of the "Miserere," the unaccompanied music becomes after a while tedious
and monotonous. On the whole, I was disappointed; and I decidedly consider the effect more
singular than beautiful. When all was over came
the dreadful crush to get out—the cruel, irreverent
crush—as dangerous as it was intolerable. I, for
my part, was completely lifted off my feet, and
found myself flung violently down into the centre
of the Sala Regia, where, by good luck, I landed
safely. The hall was exactly like the crush-room
of an opera, for the Protestant mob, as eager to
get out as they had been to get in, forgot all de-
cency in their haste. Shame on their irreverent
curiosity and stolid indifference!

To-day, Thursday, although occurring in the
midst of the profoundest mourning, is considered
by Catholics a devotional festa of joyous solemnity,
as being the day on which our Lord instituted
the Eucharist. Mass is celebrated in the Sistine
Chapel. The Pope afterwards passing in grand
procession through the Sala Regia, bears the host
to the Pauline Chapel, and places it on what is
called "the Sepulchre"—namely, the altar, which

on this occasion symbolises the sacred tomb. In the afternoon all the world throngs to St. Peter's to see the Lavandaia, which is arranged in this wise. Along one side of the transept, terminating in the chapel of SS. Processio e Martino (the gaolers of SS. Peter and Paul, who were converted by the Apostles during their imprisonment in the Mamertine prisons), on a high platform, were placed thirteen men—pilgrims, I believe— dressed in the most curiously antique costume imaginable, looking in the far distance exactly like a group of Giovanni Bellini or Francia, or some other of the early masters. They were all in white, with high conical caps, and at their back was suspended a magnificent piece of tapestry representing the "Last Supper" of Leonardo de Vinci. Why there should be thirteen apostles I cannot explain, but I can certify to the number.

After being pushed about for some time in the crowd, a general buzz, turning of heads, clashing of arms, and echoing of heavy steps along the marble floor announced the arrival of his Holiness. His throne was erected upon the altar of the adjacent chapel; and here Pius, after a short delay, appeared on a level with the mysterious apostles, who really outdid "patience on a monument" in rigid immovability. Vocal music burst forth from a hidden choir, his Holiness the while laying aside his outer vestments, and being girded by an attendant cardinal with a linen apron. He then moved towards the apostles, followed by the dignitaries of his court, while one of the cardinals chanted from the Gospel of St. John the passage describing the act of our Saviour's humility now to be commemorated. The ceremony of washing the apostles' feet occupies but a very short time. The Pope lightly touches them with a towel (after the attendant deacon had poured water on them), then stoops and kisses them; after which each apostle is presented with a nosegay.

As soon as the English ladies have seen one foot washed, they rush off like demoniacs towards the Sala Regia in the Vatican, to secure places for the Cena, which immediately follows; those who witness both being considered to have achieved a real feat of generalship. When the *Lavandaia* was over, the Pope disappeared, and I made my way along with the vast crowd into the mighty vestibule and up the Sala Regia. A more quiet, polite crowd I never beheld—all being anxious to proceed, yet none doing so at the expense of his neighbour; a silent seriousness was expressed in every face; they remembered they

were in a church, and that we had all met there
to celebrate the symbolical representation of a
Christian mystery. All honour to the Catholic
crowd after the painful exhibition of the Sistine
Chapel! When I reached the Sala Regia and
rejoined the foreigners, the Babel-like confusion
recommenced. Here thousands were struggling
and disputing, and rushing to and fro like mad.
The immense hall where the Cena is laid out was
crammed to suffocation. There were the black-
veiled ladies in enclosed seats; and in their train
the same noise, folly, and irreverence as on the
preceding day; Swiss guards trying to keep the
peace, and signally failing in the endeavour; dis-
tressed camerieri and bumptious old ladies. I
found favour in the eyes of an old sergeant of
the Swiss guard by addressing him in German:
he forthwith took me under his wing, and led me
on until I was placed close to the bar separating
the audience from the space appropriated to the
Cena. Here I saw capitally. A long table was
spread with fruit and sweets, and elegantly decorated with high vases of flowers, superb pieces
of plate, and thirteen statuettes of the apostles.
Around sat the mediæval gentlemen, who by some
miracle seemed to have been removed from the
basilica below and placed here. The Pope, simply

dressed in white, his benignant face beaming with that placid smile peculiar to him, moved quietly about the table, without fuss or effort. I remembered Abraham and the angels as I looked on the heavenly expression of his countenance, and thought that he too might be worthy to entertain "an unbidden guest" unawares. "The servant of the servants" of God was the distinguishing title of one of the greatest popes who ever sat on the throne of St. Peter, and Pius is really worthy of that touching appellation. The ceremonial of the Cena was very simple. He first bore water to the apostles in a silver basin; then, after the "Benedicite," bishops and prelates, advancing from the end of the hall, presented to him various dishes, which he handed to the apostles, pouring out water and wine at intervals. The gentle anxiety with which he anticipated their wants was inexpressibly touching. He was evidently wrapped in mental devotion, and was only alive to the outward scene as far as it assimilated with and assisted his thoughts. Never when encircled by all the gorgeous pomp of his splendid court, crowned with the triple diadem and glittering with jewels, had the Pope so much impressed me.

The office of the "Tenebræ" again takes

place this evening in the Sistine Chapel, when
the altar is divested of every ornament; the very
carpets and hangings are removed; the Pope's
chair is left without a back or a morsel of cloth
on which to place his feet; the altar is hung
with black; the crucifix is covered; and six candles
are alone left to light up the doleful scene. Not
wishing to encounter the crowd, I did not enter
the Sala Regia until so late that I found it almost
empty, every one having pressed into the portal
or on the steps of the Sistine Chapel, from whence
the soft wailing of the voices floated dreamily in
the air above the hum of the pent-up thousands
standing between me and the choir. At the opposite extremity of the hall a waving drapery un-
dulated before the door of the Pauline Chapel,
and a twilight of half-discerned stars, faintly lit
up the surrounding darkness. Drawing aside the
curtain, I entered. All was in the deepest, the
most solemn gloom, save the altar or sepulchre
as it is called, around which knelt a dark circle
of almost invisible worshippers. But that illuminated sepulchre, how can I find words to describe
its dazzling splendour? Never did the hand of
man more bravely symbolise the immortal glories
of the divine tomb than in this stupendous mountain of glittering light. Mounting to the lofty

ceiling, extending on either side in circles and clusters, and festoons of countless lights, there it rose, a glimmering, quivering, overwhelming mountain of brightness. The effect was thrilling. Tears rushed into my eyes, and Protestant though I am, *I* too knelt in the dark circle beside the glittering sepulchre, and remembered with awe the sacred symbol that rested within!

Afterwards I descended into St. Peter's. The portals were thrown wide open, and a few pale torches planted up the central aisle made darkness visible. The grand skeleton of the building alone emerged from the gloom, vast and boundless as the firmament, but a firmament unlit by moon or stars, and wrapped in everlasting night. The clustered pilasters, the colossal statues, loomed out in dim masses—gigantic forms, dreamy, fabulous, vague, fading away in fathomless distance. Here and there a momentary ray of light glimmered from the torches, was visible for a moment, and then melted away and was gone. There was something quite terrific in the scene, linking the mind to the wildest visions of chaotic gloom. Yet, even in this utter darkness, one bright symbol cheered the Christian; for, concealed behind the massive pilasters supporting the cupola, a flood of light burst from the illuminated sepulchre, shining like a beacon, and beckoning the soul onwards through the dark valley with the bright hope of immortality.

At midnight we went to the convent of the Sacred Heart on the Pincian Hill. The door was cautiously opened by one of the French *religieuses* by whom the convent—an educational and charitable institution—is conducted. She scanned us long and inquiringly as we stood on the threshold, but knowing my voice, at length admitted us. We crept softly into the church by a side chapel, not to disturb the solemn service which had already commenced. The church, a large and well-proportioned building, was dimly lighted. Many worshippers knelt on the marble floor; some were almost prostrate before the altar; others, with clasped hands and streaming eyes, lost in prayer. I never beheld a scene where such an *abandon* of religious enthusiasm prevailed. The midnight hour, the darkened church, the affecting recollection of the awful event which they had met to commemorate, seemed present with all. Service was going on; but no word was spoken, either by the priest or by the congregation—not a sound, save a stifled sigh, broke the silence. Behind the high and solid iron bars, forming a screen between the body of the church and the *sanctum sanctorum* of the high-altar, seats were placed. Presently a dark-robed, white-veiled figure glided noiselessly in; another and another rapidly followed, each taking her place opposite the altar. Now a group would emerge from the recess behind the altar, then a single figure, and again a whole cluster of black forms, passing on like a vision of shadowy ghosts. It was all so dreamy and unearthly I more than once passed my hands across my eyes to make sure that I was awake.

Such was the number of white-veiled nuns that went floating by, that an hour had elapsed before they were all assembled. The front of the altar and the steps had then become filled, the richly-robed priest, his face turned towards the altar, standing in the midst. The awful stillness grew at last positively oppressive. One by one this sombre throng received the eucharist, bowed to the altar, and retired as noiselessly as she had entered. When all were gone, the priest turned towards the kneeling congregation, who advanced to the screen and received the sacrament. I never shall forget that night; it rests on my memory like a peep into the very courts of heaven.

Although launched in the midst of the Holy Week, I must delay no longer to chronicle a happy day we spent last Monday, for fear the glowing impression should diminish.

I had heard much of the beauty of the *Pineta*, or pine woods of Castel Fusano, and I wished also to see Ostia, out of reverence for its classical associations. I do not care what antiquarians say. I throw down my glove to all of them. I can read Virgil as well as they, and I never will believe that Æneas landed at Porto d'Anzio, or anywhere else than at Ostia, where the localities so exactly tally with Virgil's description. So an excursion to Castel Fusano was arranged, which was to combine the delights of luxuriant Nature and classic memories—food for the head and the heart, not forgetting the poor body, which was cared for in a large basket, stowed away under the seat of the carriage: for the ethereal essences of our immortal being would have cut but a poor figure during a long spring day without the assistance and support of those much-abused but necessary accessories.

We left Rome by the Porta San Paolo, otherwise Ostiensis—one of the most picturesque entrances into the dear old city, rebuilt by Belisarius—flanked by the pyramid of Caius Cestius and the high turreted walls and towers beyond. And now we are driving along Tiber's banks into a pathless wilderness of green, with nothing but the white mass of the Pauline Basilica to break the monotonous lines.

We were a quartet, S. W—— again standing for Sculpture in a very pleasant form, and K——s for Architecture; and C——, fresh from England, and myself; all enthusiastic, full of fancies and wild theories; so well crammed, indeed, with Virgil and the graceful legends of old Greece, that we were little better than pagans for the time being. We first began by talking ourselves hoarse about architecture; then we as rapidly discussed sculpture; and at last, tired of chattering, settled down quietly to look at the Campagna. The soft morning air came balmily breathing across the aromatic turf, bearing rich odours of sweet herbs. Oh, those everlasting long lines! there they are again—the never-ending battle-fields I had so often traced, and of which the Campagna is literally a perpetual repetition.

Below is the broad open valley where one host lies encamped; above, the steeply-rising, undulating hills where the enemy waits entrenched, to be scaled and taken ere the day is won, and the audacious Carthaginian or the savage Gaul driven back to whence he came. Over and over

again the same scene occurs, especially in the
lower parts of the Campagna, where the early
conquests of the infant state were most fiercely
contested. The sun shone brilliantly on that
gracefully undulating plain leading down to the
Hesperian strand; the birds skimmed rapidly over
the verdant ground; and the classic Tiber, along
whose banks we drove, curved and circled in
many windings, now forming an island, now
skirting a low wood, the reedy sedges rustling
under overhanging trees. No snake ever lay more
unquietly in the sun than does that broad river
writhing across the plain. Sometimes we could
discern three separate curves, the alternate strips
of land and water lying terracewise before us, the
broad belt of the Tyrrhene Sea circling all like
an azure zone.

"How beautiful!" exclaimed K——s, as the
sea first came in sight. "It would be worth coming from England only to see this view."

On the grassy green expanse, in the valleys
and up the rifts of the hills, grew thousands of
snow-white lilies, shooting up from masses of
waxy leaves. They were unlike any other lilies I
had ever seen—so grandly beautiful, with a certain weird look, as if the fairies met under their
shadow on moonlight nights to dance fantastic

measures, and hold trysts with their sisters the butterflies and bright-winged beetles. These stately flowers could tell, I am sure, many a tale of Oberon and Titania and their tiny court when they hold high revel under the moonlight in still summer nights. Beside the lilies grew the purple Judas-trees, shedding thousands of ruddy leaves to the breeze. We were such children that we jumped out and filled the carriage with flowers, assisted by an old beggar who implored us, "by the tears of the Madonna," to give him a *bajocco*, in return for which he wished us all in paradise —a wish in which we, sinners as we were, being very happy on earth, profanely did not join.

Sixteen long miles lay between Rome and Ostia — the very voyage the "goddess-born" Æneas undertook when, warned by the god Tiberinus of impending danger, he committed himself and his companions to the "azure current." After we had accomplished the first half of the distance, we lost sight of "the noble river that rolls by the walls of Rome," and entered a woody copse. Straight as an arrow the road cleaves the low trees, until, gradually descending, we at last emerge, after many miles, on a lonely desolate region, neither sea nor land—sandy, uncultivated barren, indicative of sea, but with no sea visible

—a repulsive, melancholy scene, rank with weeds and reeds.

K——s, who had just arrived from London, was wild at having his romantic ideas so rudely scattered. "What!" cried he, "is this Ostia— the cradle of Rome—the harbour where the 'Dardanian chief' landed—where he won and wedded the daughter of the Latin king? What a sin!— what a shame that it should be allowed to sink into such undignified ruin! One can neither see the river nor the sea—abominable!"

I was, by experience, somewhat accustomed to these disappointments, Italy being a country in which I had often philosophised on Juliet's theme of "What's in a name?" This, then, was the once beautiful Ausonian shore, girt by the Tyrrhene Sea, "where Æneas descried a spacious grove, through which Tiberinus, god of the pleasant river Tiber, with rapid whirls and quantities of sand discoloured, bursts forward into the sea. All around and overhead various birds, accustomed to the banks and channel of the river, charmed the skies with their songs, and fluttered up and down the grove. Thither he commands his mates to bend their course and turn their prow towards land."

"And now," said K——s, who had read to us this passage from Virgil, "'the Lydian river' that skirted Etruria's frontiers has disappeared, the groves are cut down, the birds have turned into croaking frogs, as noisy as if just transformed by Latona, and only the discoloured salt and all-choking sand remain. I wish I had not come."

But I, for my part, rejoiced to see the spot identified with Virgil's fabled hero, however changed by the accumulated sand of so many centuries, and notwithstanding the undeniable fact that the present *paese* of Ostia was rebuilt by Gregory XIV. at a distance of more than a mile from the ancient city. One therefore looks in vain for any fragments of King Latinus's old town, where he ruled in everlasting peace; the stately palace of Picus, raised on a hundred columns, and containing the statues of the ancient kings, Italus, and Sabinus, and old Saturn, "planter of the vine," and double-faced Janus. Gone, too, is the temple where the virgin Lavinia kindled the holy altars, and gone the ancient elms on the banks of the Sacred Stream, where the milk-white sow farrowed her litter of thirty young. Really, allowing for "poetical license," and with all possible respect for Virgil, I do think it was a very impertinent thing for the newly-arrived Æneas to begin building a city without even asking leave; and so good old King Latinus seemed to think also, when he saw them marking out the walls and trenches.

The once "Hesperian strand" is now inhabited by swarms of the most unpleasant beggars draped in filthy rags, with pale, fever-stricken faces. These squalid inhabitants of modern Ostia gathered round us as we halted by the side of the gate, under the shadow of a fine old mediæval tower.   A barefooted Franciscan friar, bearing a wallet, came and begged too; and troops of old women, as hideous as "baleful Alecto" when she rose from hell to torment the soul of Amata, clustered round our carriage, the classic distaff in their hands.

The road from Ostia to the famous pine forest is such a mere track, so rough and rugged and sandy, bordered by such ditches and holes, that it would be impracticable for a carriage anywhere but in Italy.   The horses contrived, however, after immense efforts, to drag us through. At one moment we were hoisted on high, then we rolled down into the depths of a mighty rut, jolted and shaken to death.   On either side of this primitive road extended luxuriant, unenclosed corn-fields, stretching away towards the woody distance we had traversed—a rich and fertile prospect, extending to the foot of the Alban Hills, where many towns and villages dot their purple sides, while above tower the loftier mountains of the Abruzzi. The pine wood was bounded by a stagnant canal, whose unwholesome waters had become an aquatic garden. Gigantic reeds overmantled tangled masses of white and yellow water-lilies, meadow-sweet, and other sweetly-scented flowers. A moment more and we were within the deep shade of the solemn pine wood. No underwood or shrub broke the smooth level of delicate turf, or impeded our view of the lofty knotted trunks which so bravely supported their superincumbent masses of sombre foliage. Mysterious trees these, with murmuring branches that whispered, as it seemed to me, of far-off ages, when Feronia ruled the woods. An aromatic perfume scented the air, the natural incense Nature flings around her altars. Yes, this pine wilderness was beautiful.

Not far from the entrance to the forest stands in a spacious opening a castellated villa belonging to the Chigi family, interesting as the former site of Pliny's Laurentine villa. It is a residence and a fortress, the solid square pile flanked by turreted towers and loopholes, while above rises a central campanile, at once a citadel and a belvidere, for enjoyment and for defence. In our civilised age, and in a season of profound peace, such precautions may appear excessive, but situated as this villa is in a forest so near the sea, exposed alike to the attacks of banditti and pirates, they are far from being unwise or ridiculous.

Before the casino or villa, on a grassy plateau, stands an altar surrounded by woods, a fit shrine to Picus or Faunus, or the nymphs and dryads who rove within these sacred shades. Here on the velvet turf the priests about to sacrifice to the sylvan deities might have lain on outspread sheepskins, and slumbered through the sable night, waiting to commence their rites when the Aurora's shining feet first trod the threshold of the morn.

We turned into a lofty avenue of ilex, leading by a broad straight way paved with lava blocks towards the sea. Not a single shrub or tree of living green varied the peculiar colouring of these sacred woods, which stretched far away, dark, solemn, and mysterious; the distant waves softly murmuring beyond. It was a scene as of another world—calling forth other centuries and other races, and invoking an old poetic faith to people its recesses. We did not talk together, so unreal and strange was the solemn enchantment around. The ground was thickly overrun with rosemary, as in the time of Pliny (the delicate blue blossoms loading the slender stalk), flowering daphne, wild myrtle, Venus's plant, and other aromatic herbs and shrubs, perfuming this temple of the sylvan gods, whose roof was the unclouded heavens, upheld by countless pillars of the rusty pine, leading away into colonnades and naves, shrines and sanctuaries of unspeakable beauty.

I can scarcely describe the strange fancies that haunt me among the evergreen pine and ilex woods of Italy, where a funereal veil, beautiful as night, descends over the radiant face of verdant Nature; for as night is to day, so are the dark shades of those solemn trees to the bright garish colouring of other forests. It has been said that there is a philosophy in the trunks of trees. The strange contortions of the olive, gnarled and knotted by the growth of centuries, have been instanced as displaying every phase and development of human passion—the grim, morose old man in hoary trees bowed with age; triumphant youth in the stalwart sapling, strong, and fresh, and vigorous, amorously wooing the soft breezes; the growing wrinkles and coming anxieties of middle life marked in the aspect of another still vigorous tree that yet waves aloft its ample boughs of bluish green, loaded with black fruit. But, for my part, I see nothing so characteristic among Southern trees as the ilex and the pine, which are formed by Nature as if to express human passions. Dante himself must have been sensible of these picturesque associations when he represents the Harpies as wailing among the branches of dark pines, and ever and anon displaying their horrid faces from amid the foliage. To-day there was a heavy sighing sound in the wind as it passed over the pine-tops that recalled to me this poetic image. A mysterious fear came over me. I would not for worlds have plucked one of the branches that lay across our path. I am sure blood would have flowed, and that I should have heard the melancholy groan of some imprisoned spirit crying out, as did Piero delle Vigne in the "*Inferno*," "Why pluckest thou me?" ("*Perchè mi schianate?*")

Lovely as it was to wander through the woods and weave unnumbered fancies under their classic shade, the hour warned us to proceed, and we returned into the majestic avenue leading to the

shore. Beyond the forest lay a sandy belt over-
grown with low fir trees. We mounted a little
sand-hill, and behold, there was the glorious
ocean, its azure waves breaking on the yellow
strand at our feet! Magnificent beyond imagination, beyond expression, was that burst. The
boundless sea came before us like a newly-created
element, glittering with beams of golden light, its
deep blue waters putting the very heavens to
shame. Not a ripple furrowed the surface of the
deep, the water just broke in a creamy fringe
against the tawny shore, and the dark lines of the
Laurentine forest stretched far away towards
Ardea, along the Circinian strand.

Old Neptune held his court to-day, and all
Nature combines to do him honour, as in the bygone time, when Dolphin, radiant in gold and
azure scales, bore his amorous message to Am-
phitrite, dwelling deep in ocean's caves, where
corals and pearls and sparkling shells strew the
ground, and many-hued seaweeds wave in the
blue depths.

Oh, Italy! dazzling daughter of the South,
lying like a gorgeous flower on the ocean's shore,
what visions dost thou invoke by land and sea!

But the happiest dreams must end. Our clas-

sical rhapsodies were rudely broken by discovering the lateness of the hour, and—shame to say,
spite of the goddesses and the nymphs, and the
winds and the waves—by the humiliating fact *that
we were very hungry.*   Even K——s, who had
sat spellbound in a sort of enchantment, was fain
to confess "that the poor body called loudly on
the merciless spirit to have pity on its wants."   So
we took refuge in the dreary hut of a charcoal-
burner, and discussed our Italian meal of wine
and fruit and cake in an upper chamber—a most
musty, uncomfortable place after our Arcadian
seat in the woods.

As we again approached the fine old tower at
Ostia rising so grandly out of the surrounding desolation, other recollections occurred to me very
antagonistic to the visionary worship I had been
paying to the false gods of paganism. St. Augustine,
the prop and pillar of the mediæval Church, has,
in his affecting "Confessions," irrevocably connected his name with Ostia.   It was here that he
landed on first arriving from Africa, to be in-
structed and perfected in the Christian faith, accompanied by his mother Monica, of whom he
has left so interesting a description.

It was at Ostia that St. Ignatius, the friend

of Polycarp and disciple of St. John, landed when he came from his bishopric at Antioch to be massacred in the great Flavian Amphitheatre.

It was to Ostia that Marius fled when overcome by the troops of his rival, Sylla. Stained with the blood of the noblest Romans, he fled alone; for all had abandoned the now aged tyrant. A single friend, Numerius, awaited him in a small vessel, which after many mishaps and chances bore him to Carthage.

Ostia was to the emperors a suburban watering-place. They loved to sail up and down the Tiber in regal magnificence, the whole surrounding country decked out to do them honour. Old Claudius, the stupidest of hoodwinked husbands, built the port, and amused himself by loitering here while Messalina dragged the imperial purple in the filth of Rome. Hither her accusers came, and imparted to him the astounding fact that she had publicly married another man; to which he replied, like the fool that he was, "Am I an emperor?"

And in the old times, too, there were brave pageants at Ostia, such as when Paulus Æmilius, after his conquest of Macedon and the capture of King Perseus, landed there with his royal prisoner. But I have done. I feel I am off again on my Pegasus on quite another tack, one that would carry me as far as did the gods and goddesses in the Laurentian forest.

CHAPTER VII.

The Adoration—The Lateran—Mass of the Resurrection—Trinità dei Pellegrini—An Anecdote—The Environs of Rome—Rocca di Papa —Maria—Home Scenes.

I NOW resume my account of the Easter ceremonies. All Rome mourns to-day, as mourned the Virgin before the cross of Calvary. It is Good Friday, and an awful gloom hangs over the city. Every one looks sad and melancholy; an incessant tolling of bells strikes the ear; the churches are filled with worshippers, who kneel before the denuded altars and darkened shrines with every outward semblance of sorrow and repentance. "Assume a virtue if you have it not," says Hamlet. At least the very sight is edifying, as bringing forcibly to one's mind the solemn anniversary in which all Christians join.

During the mass in the Sistine Chapel, the Pope, discarding his crimson slippers and divesting himself of his cope and mitre, descends from his throne, and advances towards the crucifix on the altar, which is veiled in black. Three times he

bows in adoration before the symbolic image of
the Redeemer's passion; then, prostrating himself,
he reverently kisses the pierced feet, which are
partially uncovered, whilst the whole choir intone
the beautiful chant, "Venite, adoremus."   Three
times is this ceremony repeated, the harmony
ascending each time in a higher key, until at the
conclusion the entire figure on the cross is exposed.   There is a dramatic yet deeply touching
pathos in this rite, calculated to conquer the indifference of the most callous Protestant, and to
make even a careless Catholic tremble.   In the
afternoon the "Tenebræ" are repeated for the
third and last time, to the same vain and irreverent auditory.   At its conclusion I went into
St. Peter's, whither the Pope soon after repairs to
adore the relics.   An immense crowd was assembled.   After a while some guards, in handsome
uniforms of blue, marched up the nave, forming
a passage for the court, the Swiss Guard, and the
Guardia Nobile.   Last of all appeared Pius, always
calm and benignant, but looking excessively heated
and fatigued.   When he had reached the Confessional (the subterranean tomb of the Apostles before the altar), he knelt at a desk prepared for
him; then, taking in his hand a printed form of
prayer, the relics were exposed from the gallery

over the statue of Santa Veronica, illuminated for
the occasion. When the ceremony was concluded,
the Holy Father rose, drew off his spectacles, put
them in the pocket of his superb vestment, and
retired, followed by his sumptuous court all glittering with crimson and gold. This ceremony
did not impress me at all.

Saturday. — To-day I went with H——ns to
the Lateran. He was, as usual, instructive and
entertaining, and eager to explain the devout
significance of all we saw. He explained to me
that the services of this day, commemorating the
resurrection, are anticipated, so as not to be
celebrated at midnight, as was the custom in the
primitive Church. "The whole service," said he,
"still supposes the time to be night. A source of
the highest antiquarian interest," added he, "is
to be found in the Catholic system of symbolism,
which has appropriated from every source most
pregnant and beautiful imagery and many typical
forms. In the mystic significance of our ceremonies we are carried back to ages of which history only preserves imperfect records—to the wild
mythology of the North, the profound mysticism
of the East, to intellectual Greece and victorious
Rome—each and all recalled by many of the external ceremonies of the Catholic ritual; for the

Church—like the sun, which absorbs all other light
—in appropriating those forms, has sanctified them
to the loftiest and holiest purposes." I need not
add that H——ns is a devout Catholic.

In the meantime we arrived at the Lateran,
where an immense number of white-robed young
priests were assembled round the high-altar, this
being the day when all the clergy are expected
to communicate. The relics of St. Paul are exhibited. H——ns, however, hurried me away to
the old Baptistery near the basilica, in order to
obtain a place for witnessing the christening.
The circular building, which is not large, was
densely thronged, the spectators being arranged
on raised seats round the centre, where the large
alabaster vase stands, used as a font by Constantine, and in which Rienzi is said to have bathed
before assuming knighthood. The heat was so
intense that it required some resolution to keep
our seats. At last the procession appeared, preceded by incense-bearers and deacons. First
came the officiating cardinal, in splendid vestments, and, following him, the two candidates for
baptism—one a Jew, from the Ghetto, a sullen,
morose sinner, who looked capable of committing
murder or sacrilege for the value of a *scudo;* the
other a young negro girl, as black as ebony, her

bare woolly head of cropped hair giving her, but for her white drapery, much the appearance of a boy. There was something gentle and devout in her countenance and bearing, singularly contrasting with the stolid insensibility of her companion, who stared round at the company with audacious eyes in a most unedifying manner. Much interest was felt for this negro girl. She had been brought as a slave from Africa to Leghorn, where she became a Christian, escaped from her proprietors, and was redeemed by that excellent fraternity the Trinitarians, which is ever on the watch at these seaports to help and protect the wanderer, the orphan, and the slave. The cardinal and deacons grouped themselves very picturesquely round the baptismal vase, and the ceremony began. Water was thrown on the head of the two neophytes. By one it was received with sullen indifference, by the other with devotional fervour. The negro girl's head was reverently bowed in earnest prayer, and she looked so deeply affected that I feared every moment she would faint.

As soon as the rite at the Baptistery was concluded, H———ns, who had been quite touched by the earnest piety of the poor negro girl, hurried me off without the loss of a moment to St. Peter's. Service was proceeding in the choir when we entered; the altar was concealed by a black veil; a low, lugubrious chant told of mourning and desolation. But at a given signal a magic change took place; the *Gloria in Excelsis*, accompanied by the organ, burst forth in a rapturous pæan of triumphant harmony; the veil before the altar was rent with a loud crash, displaying a magnificent tapestry of the resurrection of our Lord; the paschal candle (an enormous torch placed beside the altar) blazed forth; the deep-toned bells of St. Peter's rang out a joyous peal, responded to by every belfry in the vast city; and the cannon of the Castle of San Angelo boomed solemnly over all. What a rapturous burst it was when the Old World rose, as it were, to new life to greet her Saviour emerged from the tomb! A thrill, an electric shock, passed over the whole congregation. Happiness and devout joyfulness beamed in every face; loving, earnest eyes were turned towards heaven; every knee was bowed in solemn thanksgiving; while the exulting strains of the loudly-pealing organ seemed to carry up the soul in a bright stream of harmonious ecstasy. The *Gloria* was followed by a grand *Hallelujah*, chanted by the full strength of the beautiful choir; while the sculptured walls of the chapel, vaults, arches, and painted cupolas seemed actually to quiver and shake with the triumphant chorus of earth rejoicing over her risen Saviour!

The mass ended, every one turned to his neighbour, wishing him a *buona pasqua;* the canons advanced towards the officiating cardinal with the same salutation; the priests repeated it again to the canons and to each other; beautiful flowers made their appearance, and were handed among the clergy from friend to friend with the same soul-stirring salutation. We passed out into the mighty aisles of the vast basilica, where thousands were saluting each other with a like holy greeting, and again bright flowers passed from hand to hand. An air of jubilee was on every face. Altars and shrines were now uncovered; the golden lamps before the Confessional were again lighted; cannon roared in the distance; musketry sounded; military music came floating through the entrance; the bells rang joyous peals—for the new year had begun, the sacred year when Jesus rose, and it was meet and fit that earth and all her children should rejoice!

In the evening we went to the Trinità dei Pellegrini, a *confraternità* founded by that most holy man, San Filippo Neri, for those pilgrims who desire to avail themselves of the indulgences conceded by the Church during the Holy Week, *ad*

limina apostolorum. Each day during the Holy
Week hundreds of men and women arrive, and
are entertained for three days free of charge; and
every evening lay members of the association, in-
cluding all the illustrious of either sex in Rome,
assemble here, wash the pilgrims' feet, and afterwards attend on them at supper.

We ascended an interminable staircase on the
women's side of the building, situated in a close
network of narrow streets in the neighbourhood
of the Tiber, near the Farnese Palace. On enter-
ing the suite of apartments devoted to the female
pilgrims, we found ourselves in the midst of light
and life, bustle and activity. Many poor way-
farers, pale, dusty, and fatigued, were seated
round the walls, staring inquiringly at the novel
scene. They were generally of the very poorest
class, but looked neat and clean, and were habited
in the romantic mediæval dress with which ballads
and legends invest all pilgrims—namely, the dark
grey or black robe, the large cape sprinkled with
cockle-shells, the broad-brimmed hat of straw
or felt, sandalled shoes, a gourd, and a long staff.
There is something very poetical about a dress
that awakens so many romantic associations.
Many visitors were present, passing from room to
room; while the sisterhood of the convent, in

13*

dresses of grey serge and with white cowls, glided
about, contrasting well with the noble ladies,
members of the institution, who wore curious
costumes of red and black, quite as strange and
mediæval-looking as the dresses of the pilgrims
themselves. What lovely faces I saw! what aristo-
cratic features, brilliant eyes, and classical heads!

After a time the great crowd of visitors had
collected in a long gallery, where, behind a railed-
in space on either side, the tables were spread
for supper. Here we waited until the press would
allow of our descending to the apartment where
the feet were washed. An old lady, the Countess
M——, emerged from the crowd, leading forward
her niece, a lovely girl, affianced to the wealthy
Marquis D——. "My niece," said the countess
to my friend Madame L——, who, habited in the
lay costume, stood near, "*vuol far qualche opera
di misericordia:* may she assist?" Whereupon
Madame L—— assented, and the beautiful girl,
smiling and blushing, was arrayed in the prescribed
dress of black, with great red sleeves and apron,
and led away below to wash dirty feet, happy as
a queen. After a due proportion of scuffling,
crushing, and pushing (for many English were
present), we also descended.

In the lower room sat between fifty or sixty

most miserable-looking pilgrims, their feet and
legs begrimed with travel-stains.   To my thinking,
these appeared ten times more wretched than
those I had seen above, but it might be that the
strong light thrown on them from the lamps
brought out all their soils in high relief.   Their
feet—but I will spare your feelings by not further
mentioning them—rested on the edges of wooden
tubs of hot water; their stockings, shoes, or sandals
were laid beside them; the noble ladies knelt by
the tubs on the bare brick floor, their white arms
uncovered, their beauteous heads bowed down,
waiting the signal to begin.   When all was ready,
a cardinal in full dress appeared, and, standing
in the centre of the room, read a Latin prayer.
While he read, the washing began, and sure such
rubbing and scrubbing and eager anxiety were
never seen.   I passed round and saw them working with right good-will, their white hands and
arms dabbling in the dirty water, and contrasting
very strangely with the sunburnt skin of the poor
women, who seemed, on the whole, quite shocked.
Others, however, looking on it in its proper light
as an act of devotion, repeated *Aves* and *coronas*.
Some endeavoured to assist, and were not permitted by the pretty ladies, who would do all
themselves; and some sat staring stolidly, over-

come with astonishment. There was the R——,
the haughtiest princess in Rome, hard at work, a
little coronet of gold just visible in her coal-black
hair; and the Marchesa C——, the most zealous
of English converts; and the sweet bride-elect
whom I had seen above so anxious to assist. No
one can describe the grace and gentleness with
which the latter performed her revolting duty.
When she had satisfied her conscience by a most
vigorous washing, she stooped down, kissed the
pilgrim's feet, drew on the coarse stockings and
the clumsy, dirty shoes, and then rose. The poor
contadina, evidently quite touched by her great
beauty and kindness, invoked an audible blessing
on her. "*E un vero angelo di beltà, una santa di
Dio,*" added the woman, loud enough for the
whole room to hear; whereupon all the bystanders
turned and looked, making the gracious bride
blush redder than roses. Oh, well be it with thee,
thou fair bride, in coming years, and may the
blessing invoked on thy young head by the poor
pilgrim be chronicled in the courts of heaven!

I can give no account of the service on
Easter Sunday, for I was too unwell to attend the
high mass at St. Peter's. Truth to tell, I am glad of
the excuse, for I hate to describe what everybody
has seen. Instead, I will note down an anecdote.

Lady C—— (who, as Mrs. Grundy said, had enjoyed herself in her day), when she was old and frail, set up her tent in the Eternal City, where she lived like a real princess. By some chance she rented the magnificent Barberini Palace, the place where the lovely Cenci lives enshrined in the picture-gallery. How, or why, or wherefore, those haughty magnates condescended to let their vast ancestral palace I cannot tell; but certain it is they did so, and that for many years her ladyship lived there like a fairy queen, for she was of extremely diminutive stature. She gave dinners to artists, who condescended to patronise her in consideration of the grand banquets they enjoyed in the old feudal halls; she had many gentlemen friends, but no female ones; she had a suite of attendants, servants, *maestro di casa*, pages, women, men, and boys— like an Eastern Begum; and she had also a *scopatore*—a humble sweeper of those gilded saloons, a common Italian *canaglia*, who seemed to have as much connection with his be-satined and be-jewelled little mistress as I with Hercules. Nevertheless, strange things do happen, and it is on the countess and the *scopatore* that my tale hangs.

She was given to purchasing ornaments,

bronzes, cameos, antiquities, and other beautiful things for the adornment of her sumptuous apartments. Well, all at once, one thing was lost, and then another, and, what was worse, the things never turned up again. My lady threatened the *maestro di casa* that if the articles were not reproduced she would sweep her palace of all her domestics as clean as the *tramontana* sweeps off the falling leaves in autumn.

"*Sua excellenza*," said the man, "you are not the only sufferer; we also have been robbed of clothes and of various things."

"Whom do you suspect?" asks the lady.

"Why, to tell the truth, signora, we all suspect Rocco."

Who was Rocco? The great little lady had never even heard the name of this obscure attendant. Rocco was the humble sweeper of the marble floors of miladi's palace. Of course he was instantly to be dismissed. Rocco was to go, and he went: miladi, in her satin boudoir, never wasted a thought on that obscure lump of clay.

One night, not long after, Lady C—— lay in bed—pillowed, as such dames are, in dainty lace and fine linen—between waking and sleeping, in a half-dreamy state of conscious unconsciousness, when she heard the handle of her door turn. In a moment she was sitting up in bed. A figure entered, bearing a light—bearing, too, something that gleamed in his hand.

"Who's there?" screamed my lady.

"Rocco," replied a hollow voice.

In an instant the truth flashed across her mind: Rocco, the *scopatore*, was there, come to have his *vendetta*. He had penetrated into the interior of the palace he knew so well, and was going to murder her! Now, the little lady was not wanting in spirit—she was no coward; so, when she heard this ominous name, she first seized the bell-rope beside her, and then darted out of bed towards a door opening into a corridor opposite. As she rushed out, Rocco bounded after her, and, with murderous haste, clutched her by her night-clothes in the passage. Finding herself within his gripe, she flung herself against him like a cat, and clung to him with the agonised hold of terrified despair. A death-struggle ensued between the wiry little countess and the strong *scopatore*. The light which he held was extinguished, but, ere it fell, she saw the upraised dagger—a moment more, and she felt it ploughing the skin in the back of her neck, blow after blow, quick as they could fall. The more he stabbed (and many were the wounds he inflicted), the tighter she clung to him. As they struggled she fell against a table, and he lost his hold; at the same moment the steward—who had heard the bell ring, but had stopped to put on his clothes—appeared with a light. Rocco rushed back by the way he had come, too quickly to be caught; and the poor little countess was picked up deluged in blood, and with two of her teeth (perhaps they were false, *chi lo sa?*) knocked out.

By earliest dawn information was given to the police. An immense sensation was excited. A peeress to be stabbed in her own palace—in her bedroom—to be dead, or dying—the assassin to have escaped! All this was tremendous. Every engine was set to work to discover Rocco; every hole of the Eternal City—and the holes where the wretched and criminal congregate in squalid poverty are many and horrible—was ransacked. At last Rocco was unearthed and put in prison; further, he was tried and condemned to the galleys for life. The man had the presumption to send to the countess for money while she lay in her bed recovering from the wounds he had inflicted. And she actually gave him money. Yes, the naughty little countess, whom ladies were too virtuous to visit, sent the assassin money to cheer his weary hours in that loathsome prison. Blessings on her kind heart! Poor Rocco never went to the galleys. He died in prison, and with his last breath begged the pardon of his generous mistress.

She soon got the better of her wounds, which were but flesh-cuts, and lived to tell the story of *"her own murder,"* as she called it, as she sat heading her amply-furnished board. She told it well, and it was esteemed a good anecdote. Now she is dead, the little countess, and all that remains of her is a pair of tiny feet sculptured in marble, a monument of vanity, in the corner of a certain studio under the shadow of the palace where she flourished. But there is a register in the good angels' book that shall not be forgotten in that solemn day of reckoning when the humble *scopatore* and the dainty countess shall stand together before the Great Judge.

*　　*　　*　　*　　*

Delightful as is the climate of Rome, its very mildness renders it so exceedingly enervating and exhausting, that after a residence of six or seven months the debilitated constitution requires a change. But the question is where to go—a query not so easily answered. Perhaps no large city in the world was ever more in want of suburban resources—a want arising from the vast extent of the desolate Campagna, which clasps the city on all sides with an arid girdle. Here not a house is to be seen, neither man nor beast thriving on that unwholesome soil, which, with its deadly night exhalations, is so pernicious in summer as to drive the very cattle from their pastures. One must journey sixteen long miles by rail or road to Albano, or L'Aricia, or Frascati, before anything in the shape of summer quarters appears. What weary pilgrimages I made! What horrible dens (all the property of princes) did I behold! It was positively sickening to walk through them. Each time I returned home more and more disgusted. At last we heard of unexceptionable apartments at Rocca di Papa, which we fixed upon at once. The Rocca, seen distinctly from Rome to the right of Frascati, is a regular eagle's nest perched on the outskirts of the Alban Hills. At a distance the place looks unattainable except by an aërial railway or a balloon; but we shall see. The air is the purest in the neighbourhood of Rome, and the sea breezes come sweeping over its woods with a delicious coolness.

We have reached our *villeggiatura*, and are

—— But I must tell things in order. At four o'clock we ordered the carriage, our luggage having preceded us in a most primitive cart drawn by two great oxen. As I 'descended the steep stairs leading from our rooms, *al secondo*—those regular Roman stairs, filthy and abominable in spite of remonstrances—and looked into the recesses of the interior *cortile* (a place which, in London, would infallibly be pounced on by the sanitary commissioners by reason of its varied and most potent smells), I really felt quite sentimental, and could not bear the idea of turning my back on wonderful Rome even for a temporary absence. But this weakness yielded to anticipations of the rural beauty and historic recollections in store for me on the Alban Hills; so, wafting an adieu to the stately Pincian Hill, and giving a salute to the dome of St. Peter's and the Coliseum, we drove out by the Lateran Gate. The Campagna traversed, we mount the lower spurs of the Alban Hills, towards Grotta Ferrata. A fair and pleasant scene opens before us; cultivation reappears; there are olive-grounds bearing rich promise of fruit, and great vineyards sloping down on the sunny side of the valleys towards gushing streamlets. There is an old ruined tower high on a rugged mound, above which the hills

whither we are journeying rise almost perpen-
dicularly into the blue sky, mildly mellowed by
the approach of evening. Now we are at Grotta
Ferrata, a small village clustering filially round a
castellated monastery—a feudal pile that frowns
down over a turfy meadow, and is approached by
several noble avenues of ancient elms. Within that
monastery are Domenichino's glorious frescoes;
but—*pazienza!* not a word of description—we
must reach the Rocca. The poor horses, hot and
weary, rest for a moment before the *osteria*, a
locality where fleas abound, and *salame* would be
dressed swimming in oil—ideas which alarm us
so much that we do not descend. So an old
man comes hobbling out with a wicker bottle in
his hand, and asks if "the *excellenze* will not
drink." "No, they won't." So off he limps,
wishing us a *"buon viaggio"* with as much earnest
unction as if we were bound for the moon on
Astolfo's hippogriff. The horses having recovered
their wind, we plunge into cavernous lanes, and
along roads scattered over with huge boulders
that must have lain there since the days when
Ascanius founded Alba. But if the roads are rough,
how lovely is the matted tangle of flowers and
moss clothing the high banks on either side—
the clematis, the vine, and the fair convolvulus

wreathing every stone and branch with exquisite garlands!

This road is interminable. It becomes worse and worse, and we seem to sink deeper and deeper between the rocky banks.

"If we should meet anything—only fancy!"

No sooner are the words spoken than, turning a sharp angle, a file of loaded carts appears, bearing down on us. Now what is to be done?

"Have the grace to stop," cries our Jehu.

The drivers respond, "*Si, si;* all is well. You shall pass." (The Italians, when not provoked, are *so* polite!)

Then, after unheard-of exertions in the way of talking and screaming (for nothing *can* be done here without an immoderate amount of palaver), the oxen and the carts are dragged to one side, and Jehu, smacking his whip, proceeds.

When we at last emerged from those deep lanes we found ourselves in a boundless forest of splendid chestnuts—a rare old wood, shut in by lofty mountains veiled with the same leafy covering. Evening shed around soft tints, deepening the shadows and dimming the vistas through these ancient trees, whose silvery trunks caught the last rays of the departing sun. But most beautiful of

all was the broom, which formed a golden underwood glorious to behold. On the rising hills, in
the wooded chasms, deep in the valleys, waved
the gilded shrubs, forming masses of colour that,
blending with the bright green, were perfectly
dazzling.

A steep ascent now lay before us, and a little
opening in the overarching boughs disclosed the
Rocca, high on the topmost mountain-peak—a
grey mysterious pile, looking spitefully down, as
if mocking our efforts to reach it. It positively
looks as distant as it did from the Campagna!
How the poor horses strive to pull the carriage up
that endless hill! And so they must, for already
the stars are appearing, and the dark wood glooms
and closes around us like a vision. In a grotto
beside the road a little shrine has been raised to
the Madonna. It contains a picture of her bearing the Jesus-child; a lamp burns dimly before it,
and sheds its flickering gleam across the road;
flowers are placed near in broken cups; and a
bright carpet of yellow broom-flowers has been
spread in honour of the Virgin-mother. As we
proceed (slowly enough now, for it is almost dark)
some one suggests *brigands*, which makes us all
uncomfortable; but as no one likes to own it, a dead
silence ensues. At last we stop; we are come as

far as the carriage can take us, and must walk up
to the house—*E così buona notte!*

Early this morning I threw open the green
persiani and looked out. Never shall I forget the
thrill of rapturous delight with which I beheld that
glorious view. The very universe seemed lying
at my feet. Description can do but scant justice
to that majestic union of woods, green and golden,
that melt lovingly into plains, which in their turn
melt into a city backed by pale blue mountains.
The mountains blend in the dim aërial distance
with the ocean; and the ocean in its turn dissolves
into the heavens. Beneath me lies the boundless
measureless Campagna—a soft desert, waving, undulating, billowy, reflecting every change of the
passing clouds, now darkened with vast masses of
shade, now dancing, dazzling, in the burning sunshine—an earthly main, changeful and fitful as
its prototype the sea. There were the yellow
corn-fields, the emerald pastures, the wildernesses
of barren grass, burnt up and calcined; while
here and there rose a sombre tomb, a ruined
tower, or a columned villa. Beyond, raised on
a stately mountain-terrace, lay Rome—that great
and unutterable Sphinx-word which the last judgment only shall unfold—throned on her seven
legendary hills; here and there a bright light or

glistening point revealing some stately portico, or
dome, or obelisk—yet all vague and undefined as
that Eternity to which her existence is so mysteriously linked.

To the right, where the mighty prairie fades
into the cloudy distance, abruptly rises Monte
Soracte—Apollo's ancient home—lone and solitary, its rugged sides and the connecting mountains darkened by the Cimmerian forest, which
leads the eye on to the graceful chain of the
Sabine Hills. To the left, a line of silver struggles
through the plain, twisting and twining like a
glittering cord—the sacred Tiber flowing on towards Ostia and the sea. Oh, the heavenly
breezes that came fresh and cool as the breath of
morning! Well was it with me in this beauteous
solitude, where all Nature—land, and sea, and
air—danced and rejoiced, as if sympathising with
my delight.

Nearer at hand lay Grotta Ferrata, Marino,
and Castel Gondolfo domed and Oriental-looking,
cresting the topmost headland of the Alban Lake.
Behind me uprose the conical height of Monte
Cavo, a diadem of ancient trees waving before
the white convent on its summit; while lower
down, on the opposite side, a broad defile, once
the Latin Valley, cleft asunder the heights of

ancient Tusculum, now fertile and verdant with
the gardens of modern Frascati. As I gazed,
images of fabulous and historic Rome floated before my eyes—Virgil, Horace, quaint old Livy,
courtly Tacitus, and bitter Suetonius were here—
no shadows of antiquity, but real living men. On
this land they had lived, on these mountains they
had sung, on those plains the heroes whose
deeds they immortalised had fought and conquered. Classic history lay like a book before
me—page after page to be read in these fair lines,
these desolate valleys, and yon boundless expanse!

*　　　*　　　*　　　*　　　*

We are becoming settled in our new home,
which English readers would think passing strange.
A great gaping door opens from the street (big
enough to accommodate a carriage and six) into
a huge passage or hall, a cross between a dungeon
and a cellar, where the horses stand, and the
boys enjoy a game of *mora—un, due, trè, sempre
l'istesso.* Stone stairs, very rarely swept, mount
up various stories to a kind of Babel altitude,
each story being considered as a separate house,
having its door and bell. On the first piano some
Italians are enjoying the *villeggiatura,* dividing
their time between sleeping and eating, the latter

operation being announced by a most potent smell of garlic. Their windows are always closed, and they scarcely ever go out; so they must have a lively time of it. But I forget, there *is* something going on at Rocca di Papa, which affords matter for gossip and entertainment to the languid natives. A Contessa, brown and dried as a walnut-shell, after having passed a life of *divertimento* and made much scandal in her day, has become a widow, and now receives the tender addresses of a certain young marquis of the Guardia Nobile, who is as poor as Job, and as extravagant as the Prodigal. When his purse is light, he mounts and rides to visit his ancient Phyllis, who, with rapturous welcome, gives him no end of money and love. Both favours received, the gallant knight rides back again to Rome, leaving the venerable Contessa inconsolable until the next time his pockets want relining. "*Telle est la vie, même au fond des forêts!*"

We rusticate above in rooms unconscious of carpets, but laid down with fine scagliola floors. Sometimes we have meat for dinner; sometimes we get only brown bread and eggs; at other times, thanks to our Mercuries, the *carbonari* from Albano and Frascati, we revel in the Egyptian flesh-pots.

Besides our own *servitù* there is a mixed and heterogeneous crowd always loitering about. First and foremost comes Maria, a stalwart contadina, with the fresh ruddy look of a rustic Hebe. She carries all the water used in the house in a great brass vessel on her head, and carries it nobly, with the air and step of a water-nymph, up those long, long flights of stairs. Maria flaunts about with a red handkerchief floating from her head, her hair pierced by a silver arrow—long, and sharp, and dangerous—a weapon she can use, too, should occasion require; for a dark devil lurks in Maria's flashing eyes. Round her neck are suspended long strings of coral, giving her, as connected with the brass vessel and the water generally, a mermaid character. On Sundays and festa days Maria puts on a smart red petticoat, with green ribbons, and a gorgeous pair of purple stays, trimmed with a profusion of white lace. She has gold earrings and a cross, which *may* be taken off; but the coral I believe she sleeps in. There are dark stories about Maria, otherwise a kind, genial soul, ever ready with her sparkling smile and hearty "*Stia bene, signora.*" She is married to a brute, a species of *cacciatore*, who divides his time between wandering in the forest and drinking in the *Spaccio di Vino*, from whence it was "his custom of an afternoon" to return home dead drunk, and to beat Maria dreadfully.

Maria, who was a comely girl, and might have married better, but for an unhappy hankering after this unworthy Nimrod, bore it meekly for some time. She bore his blows in silence, shedding sad and bitter tears over her blighted love—her true and honest love. But she was an Italian. Hot fever-blood flowed in her veins; and by-and-by desire for the *vendetta* tugged like a gloomy spirit at her heart-strings. She would have vengeance—vengeance on the man who had so basely ill-used her.

The opportunity was not long wanting. Ferdinando soon staggered into their wretched hovel, royally drunk, and flung himself upon the nuptial couch (Anglicè, the only bed they possessed). Maria, in ominous silence, was awaiting his return. She rose, and taking her needles and scissors, the weapons of our sex, sat down beside the bed on which her debased husband lay wrapped in a bestial sleep, and began to sew. Yes, to sew — stitching the two sheets firmly and securely together! Her hand did not tremble, but there was a deadly look in her black eyes all the while, pregnant of evil. She sewed until Ferdinando

was entirely enclosed as in a net; then she rose
—her eyes flashing a still darker fire—and proceeded to a certain corner where he kept his guns,
and sticks, and knives. Her hand fell intuitively
on a big stiletto knife; but it trembled a little,
and was withdrawn. She paused, then firmly
clutched the largest and heaviest bludgeon there.
A Satanic smile came over her face as she raised
the heavy stick and dealt him a portentous blow;
then another and another, until the drunken man,
suddenly sobered by the pain, writhed and swayed
in agony, as he lay weltering in his blood. His
piteous cries aroused the neighbours, who came
bursting in. They shrank back appalled at the
ghastly sight; for Maria, wild with evil passions,
stood like an avenging Fury over her husband,
remorseless, unsexed, maddened. She was seized
from behind, and the weapon forced from her
grasp. Recalled to herself, she swooned away.
Her husband, when extricated from the sheets,
was all but dead. Months passed ere he recovered,
a cowed and humbled man, who shrank away
from Maria like a beaten cur. Poverty forced
them still to live under the same roof, but they
never spoke. When we came there, a year had
passed, and Maria looked jovial and happy. She
had conquered; and but for a certain dark flash-

ing of the eye, I could not have believed so dire a tale.

We have a farm-yard behind the villa—more like an English farm-yard than any I have seen in Italy; and I love it for the sake of my far-off fatherland. There are great stacks of firewood; and tribes of poultry; and three melancholy geese wandering about in search of water, which they never find; and horses that come from the woods for their evening feed; and dogs that lie all day asleep in the shade. But, after all, it is not English; for down comes quiet Michele, the serving-man, at the *Ave Maria* in the pleasant evening time, followed by a troop of grey oxen with mighty horns, and strings of mules laden with wood, and horses carrying on their backs piled-up sheaves of sweet-scented hay from the upper pastures on Hannibal's Camp. Here, too, is the hillside garden terraced with vines; and the long *pergola* (arbour) draped with young grapes, under which my children play at *bocci* in the shade; and there is a sound of low chanting from the monastery, in the wood below, when the monks meet for evening prayer.

But I have not yet introduced you to half the humours of our rock-home, the houses of which are, as it were, chained to the rock, something

after the manner of Prometheus. There are Maria's
children, who gather about the doors, and roll in
the dust, or sleep on the bare stones—hardy little
wretches, as ignorant of soap as of algebra.
Luigi, the youngest, has his mother's eyes, and
is a real little beauty, fat, and round, and graceful as a young Cupid, if he were only cleaned
from the dirt contracted during his two year's
life.   He is always to be seen flourishing a large
table-knife, threatening instant *felo de se* when he
rolls from the top of a certain flight of stairs to
the bottom—a feat he contrives to perform many
times every day.   His great delight is to sit in
the midst of the cocks and hens and the three
misanthropic geese, which come crowding round
him with an unwarrantable freedom, pecking at
the morsel of bread he is munching—a liberty he
repels by lustily screaming and brandishing his
table-knife, with a look and action worthy of an
infant Hercules.   He would swear, that urchin,
if he could speak.   Besides tumbling down
the steps, he has an immense predilection for
water, which evil passion led him vagabondis-
ing the other day into the street to the town
fountain, where he was presently discovered with
his head downwards, and his heels in the air,
almost drowned.   Great was the indignation of

Maria, who, administering a revivifying thump, held him by the heels in the air until all the water had escaped from his mouth, whereupon she brought him home crumpled up in her apron like a dead rabbit.   But the next day he was valiantly fighting with the dogs, the geese, and the cocks and hens—the same devil-may-care little imp as ever!

Luigi, it must be owned, has a pleasant enough life of it with his little sister, whom he beats *à volonté*, unless when his young aunt Filomela (a tall, well-favoured lass who counts some fifteen summers, and carries loads of bricks on her head all day to the labourers below repairing the wall) chances to catch him in a quiet corner, when she fails not to administer her practical opinion of his conduct and principles with such emphatic arguments in the shape of blows as cause poor Luigi to wake the deepest echoes of the Rocca.   A wicked little soul is Filomela, and quite up to any mischief.

But an agreeable holocaust to Luigi's feelings is shortly offered by Maria, who, rushing down at the noise, beats her sister in return, sending her off—with abundant objurgations—to carry bricks on her head.

Not to be forgotten is our landlady, the Sora
Nena, a huge, bulky woman of some forty years
old, who amuses her leisure by drinking the good
vino sincero all day. This excellent lady is distinguished by a certain unsteadiness in her legs,
and a misty, vague expression in her eyes, when
(a gaudy handkerchief flying from her head) she
descends into the yard to take the air after the
sun has set. She generally grunts out a few inarticulate words, quite unintelligible to any one
but the fowls and the disconsolate geese, which
all flock around her in a joyous chorus, and jump
on her head and shoulders—a delicate attention
she rewards with some corn. She settles down
finally near the hen-house door into a state of
drowsy unconsciousness, and faintly calls at intervals for Rosa, her maid, who at length comes
to fetch her home. Her husband, L——, the
nouveau riche, is a study in his line. He began
life as a shepherd, and either by finding a treasure
on Monte Cavo, or egregiously cheating his em-
ployers, has made an immense fortune, bought
lands and woods, flocks and herds, and become
a *grand signore*, without the wildest notion of
how to spend or to enjoy his money, except by
grinding and oppressing the poor. He has skulked
about in the woods for weeks, to escape being

murdered by those he has injured, dozens of men having sworn to take his life; as in the republican days of Roman freedom the patrician youth vowed to cut off their country's foe, the Etruscan Porsenna.

Such is the home circle in our *villeggiatura*. Outside is a street mounting up in an almost perpendicular line towards the topmost mass of rock, where a few ancient trees — scathed and worn by the winds of centuries—wave over the remnants of a fortress, once the property of the Orsini, but now a *feudo* of their deadliest enemies, the Colonna. Besieged and taken by the Duke of Calabria in 1484, and by the Caraffeschi and the Duke of Alba afterwards, this now desolate and remote ruin has often resounded to the thunder of artillery. The rock on which it stood was originally formed by vast deposits of lava from what was once a great volcano. The village is now perched on the outermost lip of the ancient crater; the ground, the banks, the rocks are all lava. Under the shadow of the mediæval citadel, the Duomo squeezes itself in on the top of the single street, its deep melodious clock giving time to the whole village, and reminding us, though *we* lie still and dream—pleasant dreams on distant mountain-tops—that the busy world still rushes on, eager, feverish, impetuous; that death and joy, hatred and love, and every changing passion still rule the passing hour in that world stretched beneath our feet.

CHAPTER VIII.

THE great sight of our savage fortress-home
is Monte Cavo, which rises, as I have said,
majestically behind the Rocca. Troops of visitors
come daily through the chestnut forest to visit
this highest summit of the Alban Mount. I was
naturally all impatience until I also had addressed
myself to the ascent. The road lay through the
fair forests that over-mantled all around, save the
grim sides of the Latin valley and the bleak
heights of Tusculum. On I went by a rough track
through that charmed wood, passing by clearings
where those dusky squatters, the charcoal-burners,
sit month after month by their smouldering fires,
undermining the magnificent old trees spared by
time from bygone centuries when Diana ruled the
woods. On I go through parting walls of lava
rock which rise like gigantic fortifications on either
hand, the stone of a ruddy glowing colour,

warmed as it were by internal fires, and ever
palpitating with a subdued heat.   How grandly
these ravines open—laced and embroidered with
a rich undergrowth of vines, clematis, and wild
roses, and diademed with sombre trees and shrubs!
Grottoes yawn in the deep sides, leading down
into unfathomable depths — perhaps to Tartarus
and the ghastly circle where Lucifer sits enthroned
amid blue fires.   The merry light is subdued and
oppressed in this mysterious pass, where eternal
twilight reigns.   After a time the defile terminates,
and I emerge into light, and life, and sunshine,
on an elevation above the Rocca.   The ever-
glorious prospect opens far and wide.   Around
me a valley, or rather plateau, appears, carpeted
with the finest, greenest grass — a great space,
perhaps four miles in circuit, bordered by low
hills, bare and unwooded, suggesting bitter,
piercing winds;—a strange, lonely region.

This plain, so singular in aspect, is said to
have been the mouth of an ancient volcano.   For
that fact no one can vouch; nor does it matter.
But it matters much to know that it was the camp
of Hannibal, where that eccentric one-eyed hero
encamped with his army during his memorable
scappata from the South, when he hoped, by
threatening the very gates of Rome, to create a

diversion in favour of Capua, then besieged by the Consuls. But the stern Romans budged not from Capua until the gates opened to receive them in triumph. Vainly did Hannibal sound his loud alarums in his camp on the Alban Hills— vainly did he, descending into the Campagna, entrench his forces on the Anio stream, three miles from imperial Rome, and skirmish with his swift-riding Numidians under the very walls. The Seven Hills heeded not—the Palladium shook not—the sacred fire burnt bright and clear, though the dreadful Carthaginian and his awful host glittered before the very eyes of the Quirites. The ground on which he stood was bought and sold in the Forum by those immovable men of brass, who knew that it was written Rome should stand as long as time endured. At the same moment a great army marched out of the opposite gates to Spain—far-off Spain—in mocking defiance, to show the Carthaginians that Rome had stout hearts and to spare, both to conquer the Pillars of Hercules, and to drive Hannibal back in shame from whence he came. Brave old Rome!

These recollections came vividly before me as I looked on the great field, formed by nature for an encampment, with its fringe of low hills, high enough for shelter, but too bare for ambuscades.

I thought on the day when Hannibal, gazing down
on the Campagna and the Appian and Nomentana
Ways stretching away towards the towers of Rome,
saw them, as I did then, glistening in the sun.
The great outlines are the same: there, in the
distance, are the Street of Tombs, the Latin
Valley, and rocky Tusculum; but the foreground
is changed — I and my pony, instead of the
Carthaginian host and the great conqueror that
led them!

Before me rose Monte Cavo, a conical peak
said to be three thousand feet above the neighbouring ocean—a lovely mountain, green and
luxuriant as an English plaisance. The road
winds up gently through the underwood and parting branches, until a purer air clothes all around
with sheeny light. Here are no fierce rocks, no
frowning precipices, no thundering streams or
crashing avalanches—all is serenely lovely, rich
and harmonious, as befits the smiling land beloved of Venus, where the Graces and the Muses
still are worshipped. A turn of the road brought
me suddenly face to face with a group of Passionist monks—pale, emaciated men—resting on
some stones by the wayside. They had been
down into the common world, and were now returning to their sky-parlour—the aërial monastery

aloft. Ascetics as they were, and weaned from all earthly things, these good monks, like true Italians, were full of courtesy. Their *abbate* hats were instantly raised as they perceived me, and a "*Buona passeggiata alla signora*" was uttered in dull, cold voices, wherein, though no mundane passions lingered, much that was kind and charitable was expressed.

As I wound round the mountain the panorama grew wider and grander. The sea, vast as eternity, outstretched into far-off fields of light and glory, melting dreamily into the vague clouds that float down to embrace it. There was old Tiber glittering across the Campagna, and the vast forest enshrouding the descending valleys, and the two sweet lakes reposing in their loveliness within umbrageous banks—that of Albano sad and solemn, ever mourning the majestic past; Nemi like a fairy-cup set in an emerald casing, so small and delicate that Titania might have borne it in the hollow of her hand, and carried it to fairy-land. Oh, the fair smiling lawns—the bonnie braes of velvet turf—the luxuriant fields of corn, like golden rivers winding amid the woods—the tufted knolls and parting rifts that opened before me! As the fleecy clouds came and went, and "waves of shadow" passed over the mighty landscape, one might deem that some goddess was moving among the woods.

Now I have reached the old Roman kerb-stones, that begin midway up the ascent, formed of great polygonal blocks, perfect and well preserved, the marks of the chariot-wheels still visible. And this, then, is truly and veritably the *Via Triumphalis*, and these stones are worn by the chariots of Rome's greatest generals, who went up to celebrate her triumphs at the Latin shrine! Here Julius Cæsar triumphed when named Dictator; and Marcellus, after his cruel siege of glorious Syracuse, when the beauty and the power of the fair Southern capital were crushed out for ever; and many other heroes whose deeds are chronicled on the classic page,—here they passed, coming from out of the great city and its pillared Forum. Many of the stones bear the letters V. N., still plainly visible, meaning *Via Numinis*. So I am fairly *en route* for heaven— even if it be a pagan one, still heaven—and I go on rejoicing; for my Pegasus (meaning my own individual Pegasus, not the quiet pony which, poor soul! cares for none of those things) gets exceedingly rampant at the very notion of mounting to the classic heavens, and meeting the whole circle of Olympus.

15*

But mortals, though favoured with visions, are ever denied fruition. Oh, ye cruel gods! why entice me on this, your well-trodden pathway, and then suddenly break away and leave me? It was unkindly done.

Here I am actually at the summit on the broad platform, and lo! a white, ugly, staring monastery and a church—all so matter-of-fact that I feel quite unhappy. And a dog barks, and a man comes out and looks askance, and begs for *bajocchi*—all on the place where Cæsar, glittering in burnished armour, offered sacrifices for a thousand victories!

There is not a vestige of the past, not a sign to lead the mind back to the great feasts of the Feriæ Latinæ, when the forty-seven cities forming the Latin confederation met in solemn conclave. Here every consul came, before departing on foreign service, to celebrate the Latin games. Fabius Maximus, before advancing against Hannibal; and Publius Scipio, who afterwards vanquished his hosts; Marcellus, before proceeding to Syracuse; Titus Flaminius, before the conquest of Greece; Paulus Æmilius, before the Macedonian war; and Dentatus after his victory over Pyrrhus. Marcellus is especially remembered as triumphing first at Rome, and then receiving the lesser triumph

or ovation on the Alban Mount. In this ceremony the victorious general did not ride in a
triumphal chariot—in fact, the narrow road was
too steep to admit of the ascent of so ponderous
a machine—nor was he crowned with laurel;
neither had he trumpets sounding before him;
but he mounted the Via Numinis in sandals, attended by musicians playing on a multitude of
flutes, wearing a crown of myrtle, his aspect rather
pleasing than formidable, and entirely divested of
war's alarms. For the flute is an instrument dedicated to joyous measures in the "piping times
of peace," and the myrtle is the tree of Venus,
who, of all deities, is the most averse to war and
violence. Indeed, the whole ceremony of the
ovation has been referred to the festivals in honour of Bacchus rather than to those in honour of
warlike affairs.

Not one stone remains of the glorious temple
of Latian Jove, pillared on a thousand marble
columns, which once crowned the Alban Mount.
Cardinal York, Vandal as he was, has taken care
of that, and removed everything tending to lead
the mind of his Passionist monks back to pagan
times. There is but one solitary bit of ancient
wall, out of which grows a wide-spreading beech
tree, old enough to have presided over the mys-

teries of Cybele, or to have looked on when Saturnian Juno descended from her starry throne to survey the battle-field where the armies of the Laurentines and Trojans stood forth in bright array.

Then I turned and beheld the goodly lands of Latium, a fair and pleasant prospect, where the whole *locale* of the Æneid is visible:—Città Lavinia, once the Pelasgic Lanuvium, seated on its pleasant hill, the birthplace of Milo, and of Roscius and the three Antonines; Ostia, where the Trojan ships first touched the Ausonian strand; Antium, now Porto d'Anzio, once a Volscian city on the Tyrrhene Sea, where Coriolanus, "standing in the palace of his enemy, vowed eternal vengeance against his ungrateful country," where Nero was born, and from whose ruins in after ages the Belvidere Apollo emerged to astonish the artistic world; ancient Corioli, now Monte Giove, whence Coriolanus, heading the Volscian legions, marched against Rome; Pratica, once Lavinium, founded by Æneas in honour of his wife, the modest Lavinia, whose blushes, celebrated by Virgil, were "as if one had stained the Indian ivory with clouded purple, or as the white lilies mingled with copious roses;" Ardea, the Argive capital of Turnus and his Rutulians, whose walls,

once stormed by Tarquinius Superbus, were after-
wards hallowed by sheltering the exiled but heroic
Camillus, who departed hence bearing the proud
title of Dictator, conferred on him by repentant
Rome; Etruscan Cære, once a city of the Pelasgi,
but named Cære by the Lydians of the Etruscan
League, whither the Vestal virgins fled, bearing
the sacred fire, when the Gauls conquered Rome;
Tusculum, proudly seated on its rocky heights,
sometimes the rival, but often the ally, of infant
Rome, a place of fabulous antiquity, whose huge
Pelasgic walls withstood the attack of Hannibal,
but fell a sacrifice to the miserable feuds of the
middle ages; near at hand Frascati, sprung from
Tusculum's ruins; and Albano, the modern re-
presentative of Alba Longa, "the Long White
City;" and domed Castello, with its castellated
palace and its azure lake; and many a pleasant
city among the Sabine Hills, where also Tivoli,
the ancient Tibur, the home of Horace, Catullus,
and Propertius, appears embosomed and belted
with olive woods.   Further on, Monte Soracte
towers in solitary majesty—Soracte, on whose
summit once stood Apollo's golden temple; and
Monte Cimino, leading on towards ancient Etruria
and the Ligurian lands.   In the centre of the
plain lies Rome, girded with the walls of Aure-

lius, no longer the luxurious capital of the Cæsars, but consecrated to the service of that religion whose noblest temple here lifts its gigantic dome against the heavens. All Italy does not boast a braver view! Would that I could fitly describe and unfold the mysteries of the classical hieroglyphics spread around! But it is given to me only to come on a humble pony, not mounted on a living Pegasus, and I can but paint in dull prose what I saw, and how I saw it.

The platform on which the temple stood—where were celebrated the Latin games instituted by Tarquinius Superbus every year at the beginning of May, the consuls and other chief magistrates going forth in procession from the city—is now occupied by a garden, where apples and cabbages grow and ripen on the soil once so fertile in Roman laurels. No woman can enter, for the Passionist order eschews us as the parents of evil and of sin; and where amorous Jupiter once ruled no woman may approach. Strange metamorphosis! But there is an outside path running round the garden wall, constructed of massive blocks of stone, spoils of the ancient temple; and through the overarching branches of a sacred grove that yet fringes this path on the crest of the summit are disclosed glimpses of mountains, valleys, hills, ravines, all solitary and uninhabited, tossed about in chaotic confusion, a green wilderness without form and void, melting into the purple masses of the Abruzzi, whose lofty peaks shut in the prospect. And then the sea peeps out again near the rock of Terracina, that beauteous portal to the land of Græcia Magna, distinctly visible in the far distance; and the small islets of Palmaria and Pandaria lie like dots on the blue ocean.

One more long look towards the great city and I am gone; for see! the sun, a ball of liquid fire, is sinking beneath banks of purple clouds, the sound of the *Ave Maria* rises from the church of the Rocca below, and the stars are coming out one by one.

* * * * *

Maria told me to look out of the window this morning, and I saw that the ground before the opposite house was strewed with rose-leaves.

"*Cosa significa?*" said I to the jolly *donna di facenda* (housekeeper) who stood beside me, bridling and looking full of mystery.

"*Significa l'amore*," replied she. "*L'amore, il bel amore.*" And she sighed and looked sad for an instant, and I remembered her rage and jealousy, and how she sewed up the unfortunate *peccatore*, her *sposa*, in the sheets.

"*Ma*," said I again, "*che cosa significa?*"

"*Ascolta*," said she. "Opposite lives the baker Pietro, he that wears the red cap. Well, he has long loved the daughter of Fondi, the pretty Teresina; but her parents said she was too young, and sent her for education to a convent for a year. To-day she is seventeen, and she has returned, and Pietro has strewed the rose-leaves before her door to declare his passion. *E un certo modo nostro.* He has strewed the rose-leaves: if they are removed, 'tis a sign she refuses his suit; but if they remain, why, *certo*, she accepts him. Ah! Teresina will not sweep away the rose-leaves, *ne son sicura.* They may fade, but her love for Pietro, and Pietro's love for her, will only bloom and blossom as time goes on. Once it was so for me, and rose-leaves were strewed before my door in the grey morning light—red rose-leaves, to show the fervour of his passion. When I went out at sunrise to draw the water, I stepped on them; and when he saw I smiled, and gathered some into my bosom—for he was hid behind a *portone* watching me—he came forth and kissed me, and asked me to be his wife. But it is all changed now. *Tempo passato non ci penso più!* But still —*che bella cosa è l'amore*—I could have loved long, yes, and borne much, *Iddio lo sa;* but——"

She pointed to the fresh rose-leaves, and tears sprang into her bright eyes. "There will be a serenade to-night," continued she, wiping away her tears with the back of her hand. "Two guitars will play sweetly before Teresina's door when the moon rises, and she will come out on the balcony to show Pietro that she is pleased and accepts his suit. Oh, *che bella cosa è l'amore e la gioventù!*"

I must introduce some more of the characters of our Rock perched up so high near the Via Numinis. We almost forget we have any relation at all with *terra firma*, and are inclined to try an excursion on the ambient air; but, although this heavenly altitude affects me with uncontrollable fits of longing to be off and away into the land of ideality, the rest living up here are of the earth earthly. The Contessa below thinks only of her knight—he of the Guardia Nobile, who dutifully comes, trotting on a donkey from Frascati, to visit the deploring fair—when he has spent all his money, *bien compris!* A little niece, some sixteen summers old, has arrived from a convent to visit her aunt. I wonder what she thinks of things in general, and how she will describe her aunt's *ménage* to the pious Sisters! Talk of Italian ladies' progress in virtue—oh, *miserere!* the sun shall stand still in the heavens, truth shall become a liar, the Ethiopian cast his sable skin, before Italians learn to practise virtue!

Then there are the geese—ah! they are far more interesting than the marchesa and her super-annuated loves. Their fate is a *real* tragedy—those unhappy birds which wandered for years up and down in search of that "something unpos-sessed" (viz., a mossy pond, such as is seen in a shady English lane, under thick hedgerows), but, withal, quiet and uncomplaining as they increased and multiplied. They are all dead as ducats! It fell out in this wise. The Padrona Nena—she who sacrifices each afternoon on her domestic altars to the jolly Bacchus god—in a drunken frolic descended with her three attendant Furies, or rather Fates. They seized the devoted birds quietly reposing on the grass, and cast them head-long into a pool of water used to irrigate the garden—a high walled-up place, from which there was no escape. There they left them, laughing and yelling like evil spirits at the frolic. The geese, unaccustomed to the cold of the chill, un-wholesome tank, struggled to escape; plaintively they cackled, and beat their snowy wings with dumb and piteous pleadings; but in vain—their fate was sealed. No more the bright August sun would shine for them—no more would they peck

the moist scented grasses under the wide chestnut
trees—no more rest under the pleasant vine-arbour
in the garden where they were first freed from the
encircling egg.   Clotho had drawn their brief
thread of life, Lachesis had turned the wheel, and
Atropos, with her fell scissors, cut the slender
thread.   The poor geese all died a melancholy
death in the cold tank.   But they died not un-
lamented, for their misfortunes caused such do-
lorous sympathy among the children, that after
shedding those bitter tears that any strong and
sudden grief so readily calls to the eyes of infancy
—after wreathing and garlanding the poor white-
feathered corpses with flowers—they buried them
under a solitary rose-bush in the garden.

But away with melancholy—it befits not our
cloud-home.   Yesterday was a festa; the church
bells rang a merry peal; little cannons exploded
from the top of the rock; and squibs and crackers
woke the classic echoes of Jove's ruined shrine.
The contadine appeared in their snowy head-
dresses, coral beads, and crimson bodices, and
said their prayers to the Madonna del Tufo (of
the Rock); and then a party of laughing maidens
came to dance the *tarantella* in our rooms.   Glee-
some, jolly maidens these, their girlish forms
already rounding into voluptuous womanhood.

Timidly they came at first, one by one, with a rough curtsey, and a *"Buon giorno, signora,"* and sat down crimson with blushes. But when Elena, the fair-haired daughter of the *speziale*, struck the tambourine with a grace worthy of Terpsichore herself, and sent out the lusty whirring sounds that the excitable Italians love so well, and little Giuletta, who had brought an harmonicon, accompanied her with some simple notes, than the bright-eyed girls came pressing through the door, all anxious to dance before the signora. They began —Carolina with Michelletta, sounding the merry castanets, and describing rapid circles round each other—now near, now distant—now accepted, now rejected—till at last Carolina kneels, and her partner dances round her in triumph. 'Twas a pity such eloquent dancing should have been wasted on a girl!

After the dancing had fairly begun, the tambourine passed from hand to hand, and many a graceful measure was threaded. Maria danced fast and furiously for awhile, as became her passionate nature, and stamped on the floor, and flew round and round with vehement energy; then, as if a vision of the past had suddenly appeared before her, she covered her face with her hands and rushed out. *"Povera Maria,"* said her forsaken partner, "*ha mollo sofferta.*" The miller's love came too—she before whose door the roses were strewn—looking conscious and happy, a trifle reserved, perhaps. She* sat in a corner and arranged her head-dress, and smoothed her hair, thinking doubtless of the miller, and of all the pleasant things he said.

After the dance they partook of wine—good *vino sincero* of Genzano, sweet and creamy, like champagne—and of *salame* and cakes; each coming to thank the signora for her *gran bontà*, and to wish her all kinds of felicity. And then the merry girls ran off; and then the tambourine was heard in the street; and then it sounded fainter and fainter as they ascended the hill, until distance bore away the sound, and all was silent.

Marino, surrounded by castellated walls and towers, picturesquely situated on a rocky height overlooking the Campagna, is a place I love to visit—a cosy, happy-looking spot, little suggestive in its aspect of the dark reputation it bears of being in its collective capacity extraordinarily addicted to the use of the stiletto. There is a mediæval look about the town that fascinates me. Here an old wall pushes forward, forcing its way through the modern buildings; there an old gateway, flanked by tottering "towers of other days," leads, perchance, up a lonely lane, where, if you value your skin, you would do well not to venture alone after the *Ave Maria*—that pathetic twilight hour the' *assassini* love so well. Whenever you hear of a robbery or a murder, it is sure to have taken place about the *Ave Maria*. The *sgrassatore* offers up his hasty prayer to the Virgin, fumbles over his *corona* (for they are all wildly superstitious), and, thus fortified, plants himself, musket in hand, under the shadow of some high bridge, or clump of trees, or dark *portone*, from whence he can take a deliberate aim at your head, unless you will freely consent to make your *meum* his *tuum* . . . . else——Heaven and all its saints have mercy on your soul!

Marino can boast broad handsome streets, where the soft summer breezes have free leave to palpitate. There is a pretty piazza, with an antique fountain rich in gods and nymphs, somewhat coated and obscured by moss, but still, even in their fallen condition, attractive. There is a fine mediæval palazzo, looking down with dignified scorn on the surrounding houses. And there is a duomo with a handsome architectural façade; to say nothing of scores of pretty women wearing long while veils. No wonder the town looks mediæval, for its history is a rare old chronicle of the feudal times. Volumes might be written of all the fights, sieges, and battles fought under its tottering walls. It was originally called Castrimænium, and is mentioned by Pliny—whether favourably or not, in regard to its acknowledged fighting and cut-throat character, I have no means of ascertaining. Then it afterwards became a stronghold of the Orsini family—those powerful barons whose ceaseless hereditary feuds with the rival house of the Colonna so often crimsoned the streets of Rome with blood. Marino was to the Orsini a mountain stronghold and an impregnable fortress, from whence they could defy the thunders of the Vatican (then weakened by distance, for the terrified popes had fled into France), or the attacks of their hated rivals. In those days the walls were manned with stout German mercenaries belonging to the great companies of free-lances, more odious to the Italians than the devil himself,—days so black, and dreary, and heavy with crime, one wonders how the miserable old world contrived to outlive them.

When a ray of light penetrated this opaque gloom, it was in the person of Rienzi, that eccentric but generous-hearted patriot, who so loved the great city which gave him birth that he endeavoured to revivify her wasted energies, and

plant about her dying trunk the fresh soil of freedom. In this noble attempt to revive "the good
estate" Rienzi was bitterly opposed by the blood-
thirsty Roman barons, who, like foul and savage
beasts, battened on the general slaughter. The
Orsini, most savage and remorseless of all, were
his bitterest enemies. Giordano Orsini, expelled
from Rome as a traitor to all law and order,
retired to the fortress of Marino, where he was
besieged by Rienzi, but the Bear of the Orsini
prevailed, and Rienzi was driven back.

In the following century, amid the chances
and changes of war, Marino passed into the possession of the Colonna, who at last, after having
sacrificed thousands of lives, and spread misery
and annihilation around, conquered their ancient
foes. "Revenge and the Colonna!" was now the
cry. "The Bear" was forgotten, or only remembered on some old frieze, or capital, or
painted sign, which the rival house had not cared
to obliterate.

Many times subsequently the possession of
this stronghold was disputed. Once it was besieged by Ricci, Archbishop of Pisa, one of those
warlike prelates who loved plated armour better
than sacerdotal robe, embroidered cope, or cup

and chalice. Again the stout fortress was attacked by Sixtus IV. But the Colonna, determined not to lose so valuable a retreat, fortified it anew with massive walls and strong towers whose ruins still remain, though overgrown by umbrageous trees and waving shrubs, which hang over the lovely valley below—a valley so narrow, so deep, so mysterious, so belted and darkened by woods, that before descending a very precipitous hill, and actually treading its cool recesses, one would never dream that it existed at all. Oh! the romantic, solitary dell, surrounded by hills broken into rocky ravines and dark fissures, all of the same ruddy sunburnt tint as the bare rocks on which the town is built. Great overarching trees of living oak, a bubbling stream that sparkles through the grass, and thick underwood mantling the hillsides unite to make it a place to dream of—cool, murmuring, delicious, while the surrounding lands are baked by the fervid sun. There is a gate beside a fountain that bursts splashing out of a wall, leading up through an overarched walk of willows to the deepest part of the glen. This is the Parco di Colonna, a labyrinth of loveliness, leading on under red rocks through wooded braes, and by lawns sown with pink and white cyclamens. After following

16*

this beauteous ravine for some time, a bluff face of tufa rock, overmantled with arbutus and acanthus plants, shuts in the path, out of whose sides the presiding deity of the cool valley, a sparkling stream, gushes forth, and falls into two shallow circular reservoirs or basins. I am particular in describing' the aspect of this spot, for the valley—which I would have you admire as much as I do—has a history—an ancient, time-worn history—chronicled by old Livy himself. The same rocks that shelter us, perhaps the ancient oaks and sombre ilex trees under which I stand, and this brawling stream, rushing from the silent woods to career in light and sunshine beyond, saw the Latin tribes assemble on the day that proud Alba could no longer shelter the confederate nations within her stately palaces. The forty-seven tribes that formed the strength of infant Rome held their triumphant festivities on the Alban Mount, whose summit tops the distant prospect, and met for deliberation in this valley—beside this stream called the Acqua Ferentina—where, under the leafy canopy, they sat in common conclave.

On a certain day, when kings ruled the seven hills of Rome, Lucius Tarquinius issued orders that the Latin chiefs should assemble at the grove of Ferentina, to confer on some matters of common concern. They came accordingly in great numbers at the dawn of day, but Tarquinius delayed making his appearance until sunset. Meanwhile, the news of the day, and various topics of general interest, were discussed by the assembled chiefs as they sat by the banks of the stream awaiting the arrival of Tarquinius, who, in thus disregarding his appointment, taught all men that he was with reason called "the Proud." Turnus Herdonius, the chief of Aricia, was loud in his complaints against Tarquinius, and eloquently resented the affront put on them all by his absence. "It was no wonder," said he, "that the surname of 'Proud' had been given him at Rome. Could any greater instance of pride be given than by thus trifling with all the nations of the Latins, after their chiefs had come so great a distance in obedience to his summons? He surely must be making trial of their patience, intending, if they submitted, utterly to crush them, for it was plain by such conduct he aimed at universal sovereignty."

This and much more was spoken by Turnus of Aricia. While he was haranguing the people, Tarquin himself appeared, and every one then turned from Turnus to salute Tarquinius, who was surrounded by his lictors and attendants—a pompous train befitting so powerful a king. Standing forth in the grove, he apologised to the chiefs for his remissness, saying "that he was obliged to remain in Rome, having been chosen umpire between a father and son;" which when Turnus understood, he was heard to mutter, "That there was no controversy between a father and son that ought not to be terminated in a few words, for that a rebellious son should suffer the consequences of his rebellion." Indeed, Turnus continued so indignant at the slight put upon the chiefs, that he retired from the assembly, leaving the rest in consultation with Tarquinius.

Now this latter was highly incensed at seeing Turnus retire into the woods, where temporary lodgings had been prepared for the chiefs; so, being a bad and wicked man, and fresh from the murder of his father-in-law, he determined to have his life. In order to affect this purpose, he bribed some Aricians to convey a quantity of swords privately into Turnus's lodgings during the course of the night; then, a little before sunrise, he caused the other chiefs to be summoned in great haste, as if he had been alarmed by some extraordinary event, exclaiming, as they entered, "That his accidental delay of yesterday was surely owing to the favour of the gods, since it had been the means of preserving him and them from destruction, for that he had been assured that Turnus of Aricia had formed a conspiracy to murder them all, that he alone might rule over Latium. He was told, indeed," he artfully continued, "that a vast number of swords had been privately conveyed to his lodging: therefore he requested all the chiefs to accompany him at once, and see if the report were true." There was a great commotion among the chiefs as they listened to what Tarquin said, and they ultimately followed him to that part of the wood where Turnus lay asleep, surrounded by his guards. His servants, observing the menacing aspect of the chiefs, prepared, out of affection to their master, to oppose their approach: but, being few in number, they were soon secured, and the swords which Tarquinius had caused to be concealed were drawn forth from every part of the lodging. Then Turnus was loaded with chains, and an assembly of the chiefs being called, and the swords brought down and laid in the midst, their fury became so ungovernable that they would not even allow him to speak in his own defence, but at once commanded that he should be thrown into the reservoir of the Acqua Ferentina—*Caput Aquæ Ferentinæ*—where a hurdle was placed over him, and upon the hurdle a heap of stones; and so he was drowned.

Extraordinary to say, after the lapse of so many centuries, Ferentina still remains precisely in its original state, being the bluff face of rock I have so particularly described, from whence the stream flows into a circular reservoir, much too shallow, indeed, to drown a man, unless he were pressed down by absolute force.

S. W—— came up the other day to pay us a visit from imperial Rome. (I feel such respect and love for the dear old city, I can never mention it without qualifying it with a majestic adjective.) Well, S. W—— came up, and underwent quite a chapter of accidents. The horse sent to meet him, being occasionally troubled by an affection of the fore-leg, was attacked with this chronic complaint on the road, and, without the slightest intimation of his intention (which, considering the circumstances, would only have been polite), dropped poor S. W—— on a heap of stones. S. W——, bruised, astonished, and indignant, refused to mount the treacherous quadruped any more, and addressed himself to the journey on foot. But as the mountain road through the *macchia* is as difficult as the road to paradise, when he arrived, what with the fatigue, and the heat, and the bruises, he was inconsolable.

The next morning it rained an Italian deluge, notwithstanding which S. W—— would ride (on another horse) through the forest, now damp as a sponge after the recent moisture. We told him he would have a return of the Roman fever; but our counsel was in vain. Off he went, and on again came the rain—a respectable waterspout. Hours flew by; the rain continued; but no S. W—— appeared—so we supposed some of the elderly English maidens abounding at L'Ariccia had taken compassion on him and housed him. Not a bit of it. Up comes a little pencil-note, saying he had taken refuge at Palazzuola, a romantic convent on the shores of the Alban Lake, and was so happy with the Franciscan monks, he didn't intend to return till the next morning. When he came back he told us all about it.

The rain driving him in, and an ominous fit of shivering supervening, the good monks were full of compassion. He was installed in the great *sala* looking out over the mysterious lake from a window with a balcony "*alla Giuglietta.*" This room, grand and spacious as a feudal hall, was lined with pictures of founders, benefactors, popes, and saints—all good and holy men, whose images seemed to sanctify the solemn *sala*.

Then they took S. W—— through long corridors lined with cells and dormitories on either hand (each bed with its little crucifix lying demurely on the sheet), down into a beautiful garden, "quite," as he said, "unreal and enchanted-looking, like fairy-land." The cypress, "the Virgin's tree," that points towards heaven, grew there in thick, tangled masses: and ilex trees, and fresh oaks, and sycamores. Long broad walks stretched across the formal grass-plots, by ruined fountains where pale lilies grew, to shady groves beyond. On one side the garden was enclosed by mediæval walls (the place is more like a fortress than a monastery even now), castellated and turreted, and carved in quaint devices, with heavy stanchions and buttresses overhanging the trackless woods that are mirrored on the bosom of the sleeping lake.

Well, on the opposite side of that antique garden, along whose front ran a lordly terrace, uprose the solemn rocks on which the building stood, moss-grown and grey with the hoary dew of centuries. There they lay, rifted and ravined, and broken into fantastic glens and crevices— here a yawning cavern, going no one could guess

where; there a hole, as deep as Malabolge; further
on, a deep, deep rift, bottomless as the everlasting
pit. Such was the garden as S. W—— described
it, with the sedate friars creeping noiselessly about,
their black robes, and monkish cowls, sandalled
feet and hempen girdles, harmonising, like a chord
of sweet music, with the impressive aspect of that
fair, sad scene.

There was no end to the *gentilezze* of these
worthy Franciscans, who, after walking him all
round and about through the vine *pergole* and up
among the leafy arbours in the rock, showed him
over the establishment, the stables, the bakehouse,
where a lay brother was up to the elbows knead-
ing flour; the kitchen where another cowled monk
was labouring among the frizzing spits, and pots,
and pans; even to the savage dog that kept the
gate. Then he saw the church, where they daily
sang their psalms of love and praise; and, in fact,
everything—ecclesiastic, mundane, domestic, romantic, feudal—in this forest-home and convent-
fortress.

When supper was ready, the monks, twelve in
number, assembled in the refectory, where stood
six little tables, each table being laid for two persons; in the centre were bread and a bottle of

padronale wine. The superior took his station at the top of the room—an eagle-eyed, sharp-featured man in spectacles, who had an inveterate habit of putting away everything into the overhanging folds of his right sleeve. At his little table was seated a friar from Assisi on a visit—a personage of importance; for, although the Franciscans are a begging order and ought to possess nothing, all the monks at Assisi are gentlemen and *possidenti*, and, as such, are much regarded by their poorer brethren. When the superior had pronounced a *benedicite* and blessed the tables, and the monks had crossed and blessed themselves, the *cena* was brought in by the lay-brethren—humble, servile fellows of the "Friar Tuck" pattern, red-cheeked, jolly, cunning-looking, and withal orthodoxly smelly and dirty. These lay-brethren, never having been ordained priests like the other monks, form the ecclesiastic *profanum vulgus*. A priest is a gentleman, though penniless, because he *is* a priest, and can celebrate mass and offer the blessed sacrifice; but these—they are the *oi pollio*. Well —speaking after S. W——, for no woman, under pain of the most horrible excommunications, can enter these doors—the *cena*, consisting of *minestra* (broth), *frittura*, or omelette, salad, roasted quails, fat and luscious, shot by Fra Felice in the wood,

and fish netted by Fra Giacomo in the classic
lake, was admirably washed down by wine—and
such wine! Ye heathen gods! had ye then left
behind a sample of Bacchus's sparkling cup when
ye fled from these your native wilds? S. W——
got quite enthusiastic about the wine, I assure you;
and said the monks, though moderate, seemed to
enjoy and value its fine flavour. One *frate*, enter-
ing after the *benedicite*, kneeled on the floor before
the superior, with his hands clasped; the superior
hotly engaged in an argument with the *possidente*
from Assisi, did not perceive him; so there he
knelt motionless, looking like a penitent ghost
come to be shriven, until at length the superior
saw him, and made the sign of the cross over
him, when the *frate* took his allotted place.

After supper all the community assembled in
the noble *sala*, the setting sun lighting up the
old walls in a glowing haze. Beyond, over the
sea and the Campagna, bands of gold and purple
clouds shone for awhile; then the blue hills melted
into grey, and the gloomy mountains darkened
into black. The window was closed, the *lucerna*
appeared, cards were brought out, and the monks
played *una partita* with the well-thumbed packs
which had afforded amusement to many a genera-
tion of tonsured friars. At length, when night

was come, they made up a bed for S. W——in
the great *sala*, where he slept soundly, under the
custody of those stern old images looking down
from the walls—the guardian angels of the place.

———————

CHAPTER IX.

A Hot Day in Rome—Sunsets—The Tramontana—Classical Recollections of Albano and Castello—The Festa of the Madonna del
Tufo—Characters.

PEOPLE have an idea that the Italians are becoming more civilised and eschewing the use of
the stiletto; that a Bravo is a chimerical animal
only existing in Cooper's romance; that wives are
virtuous, husbands faithful, and cicisbeism quite
out of date and altogether ungenteel. All these
charitable surmises are mistakes—I could recount
various anecdotes proving the truth of what I say
—but as to the murdering part, listen. There
was a day last week in Rome of intense heat. I
suppose this state of the atmosphere occasioned
a moral delirium, for many who rose that morning
blithe and gay, lay down before night on mother
earth never to rise again. There was a madness
abroad that day for certain.

S. W—— and a friend were refreshing the
outward and inner man by a siesta at Nazzari's

and an ice, when their attention was attracted by
much running to and fro, loud talking, swearing,
and tumult—a general excitement, in fact, all
tending towards the Via Babuino. They joined
the crowd, and heard that an *assassino* had been
committed in broad daylight, and that the corpse
lay there. Pressing forward, they saw extended
on the stones, quite dead, a lovely girl weltering
in her blood, with a deadly wound in her side.
They at once recognised her as a well-known
model, renowned for her beauty and grace. There
she lay, pale and bloody, on the cold stones,
until some of the brothers of the Misericordia
came (they that wear the black masks and long
dark robes, and look more like mummies than
men) and composed her limbs, and, laying her
in a great sheet, carried her away. She had been
walking with *un certo amico*, it seems, in the Via
Babuino, when her husband passed. His ire was
kindled, his jealousy aroused; he drew his stiletto
and slaughtered her there on the spot where she
stood; then ran away. But the *certo amico*, her
cavaliere, ran after him, and watched and dodged
him into a certain house; and when in the evening he came out, the said *amico*, having his stiletto
ready hid in the sleeve of his coat, struck him
down then and there, and left him lying weltering

in his blood as she had lain. Whether this valiant lover escaped or not I cannot say.

That same day a man was passing in a cart through the Piazza Barberini, where Bernini's classic fountain plays in the sun. Some one crossed his path, and, being nearly run over by the *carettino*, gave the horse a blow with a stick. No word was spoken; but the *carettiere* stopped his cart, descended, deliberately drew his stiletto, and stabbed the man dead; then, remounting, drove away. So much for the effects of a hot day in Rome.

We have had a series of the most magnificent sunsets imaginable. Sometimes great bands of purple and gold clasp the broad horizon in gorgeous girdles, the gold melting into the ocean in fields of glistening fire, or flaming here and there upon a distant mountain-peak, all Nature lying dark and black as a pall—a fitting foreground for this brilliant sight. Sometimes the whole heavens seem on fire—a terrible conflagration prefiguring that awful End when the earth and all that it contains shall be consumed with fervent heat. I have almost trembled as, standing under the *pergola* in our garden, I have watched the awful scene, too horribly beautiful to contemplate with aught but dread. Golden clouds, dissolving into crimson,

saffron, and starlet, lay quivering and palpitating
as in an atmosphere of ardent fire, save when here
and there sombre masses of purple, tipped with
the prevailing fire tint, bore storms and thunders
in their deep bosoms. Anon the parting clouds
opened into cavernous recesses of inmost glory,
and the sun, an orb of liquid fire, glowed out
"stern as the unlashed eye of God." For awhile
it glowed in infinite light, irradiating the sad
Campagna with a wild, unearthly hue; then, dipping into the encircling sea, it slowly vanished,
deep shadows fell fast around, and the sullen,
purple, massed-up clouds turned into banks of
sombre lead colour. I have seen the sky at other
times completely covered with a network of purple
and gold, with here and there touches and tinges
as of fire, while between the parting rifts pale
blue sky peeped softly out; and I have seen the
vaulted firmament of a sweet heavenly blue, as it
may have looked when God beheld his labour and
pronounced it good.

Then, after the sunsets, came a mighty wind,
the Tramontana, down from the icy North, passing across the snowy summits of the everlasting
Alps, and bearing in its breath biting frosts
from their glacier bosoms—a furious wind that
tore and rent the gigantic trees, wrenched the

mantling leaves in showers from the bending boughs and thundered among the rocky caverns of our hills like a torrent of invisible avalanches.

How that Tramontana wind roared and whistled about our mountain home! How it raged up at Monte Cavo! Heaven help the poor monks! They must have trembled in their beds, and said many an *Ave* in their fear. How it yelled among the tottering ruins of Tusculum, and bent and twisted the grand old pine trees that diadem its sloping woods around Cicero's ruined portico! The motionless waters of the Alban Lake swayed to and fro this wild and dreary night—those mystic waters that never listen to the enticing breath of fragrant summer. Even Nemi, too, Diana's mirror, must have lashed its wooded sides under the influence of such a hurricane.

I thought of all this sitting beside the blazing wood fire on our own cheerful hearth, while the storm raged remorselessly without. It is delightful to sit and listen to the shrill whistling of the gale; to watch the shadows on the wall as the fire flickers. There is an exquisite sense of luxury and domestic peace and household security at such a time. There I sat; and I questioned the wind as it swept up from the far North, of many things. I asked it of a certain corner in a certain room which it used to love of yore, in the spring-time, when its breath came perfumed with the year's young flowers; and the answering wind, always loud and shrill, told me that strangers dwelt there now, and that since the days of my joyous girlhood none had cared to hearken to its constant sighs in that familiar room. "Ah, wind!" cried I, "but you were false, for there you pro-phesied such pleasant things."

I have endeavoured to describe the classic valley of Marino. An ascending road through a magnificent wood leads from the Acqua Ferentina towards Castello and Albano. On emerging from the wood the Alban Lake bursts on the sight, its sullen waters unruffled by a wave. In front, Monte Cavo rises majestically towards those clouds to which its Via Numinis professes to lead. To the right Castel Gondolfo stands on a grand natural platform overlooking the lake, quite embosomed in dark poetic woods. I have already said that the shores of this lake are strewn with ruins, the foundations of former nymphæums and grottoes, while pillars, marbles, and mosaics are perpetually found among the surrounding woods.

The grandest of the imperial villas was that erected by Domitian on the spot now occupied by the Villa Rospigliosi, near Castel Gondolfo.

To-day I rode all over this district, and, finding
the gates of the villa invitingly open, I entered
the gardens, which occupy the fall of the hill between Castel Gondolfo and Albano.   Long avenues
of ilex trees terminate in lovely vistas over the
Campagna, melting away in blue distance towards
the sea, and are here and there diversified by
groups of antique statues, vases, and pillars wreathed
with vine and clematis.   The Rospigliosi gardens
boast a terrace-walk more than a mile in length,
entirely formed by overarching ilex trees—a majestic avenue, fit only to be trodden by the great
ones of the earth.   Midway along this ilex avenue
are the ruins of Domitian's palace—indistinct
masses of wall, without form and void, and wholly
overgrown by ivy and other plants.

Standing before those misshapen ruins, it
seemed scarcely possible to call forth a vision of
the palace erected by that deified monster whose
reign disgraced the annals of the Flavian line; yet
on this spot, and descending towards the lake,
stood one of the loftiest piles that even antiquity
can boast.   Here were magnificent atriums; great
vestibules; halls of almost fabulous extent, supported by columns of the rarest coloured marbles,
and adorned with Grecian statues; ceilings and
walls painted in brilliant fresco that harmonised

in colour with the patterns on the mosaic floors, and were supported by cornices of silver or of gold; temples glittering with gilded plates; marble colonnades stretching through the surrounding groves; fountains of perfumed waters springing from parterres of brilliant flowers; Odeons for music and song; vast baths, where, under gilded roofs upheld by crystal columns, the cool water flowed into alabaster reservoirs; magnificent porticoes, leading by flights of steps down to the lake, where, beside the deep waters, grottoes and caves, decorated as tricliniums and nymphæums, were dedicated to the water-nymphs, the presiding deities of these enchanting shores.

But the circus and the amphitheatre attached to the palace were most frequented by Domitian himself. Here he was constantly present, wearing a golden crown and robes of purple, and surrounded by the priests of Jupiter and the Flavian College. Not only men but women exhibited themselves in the gladiatorial games, and ran races at night under the glare of the torches with which the amphitheatre was illuminated. Even torrents of rain did not deter Domitian from remaining until the conclusion; he himself frequently changed his clothes, but a positive law forbade the audience to leave their seats. The Lake of

Albano afforded an admirable *locale* for the naval
battles in which he also delighted. Suetonius tells
us that he regularly celebrated the festival of
Minerva here, for which purpose he established a
college of priests on the Alban Mount.

Born with a mean and cowardly nature, Domitian, conscious of the hatred he excited, trembled
at his own shadow, unless surrounded by his
guards. We are told that he daily shut himself
up alone in the interior of his palace, for the purpose of killing flies with a gold bodkin! Sometimes when visiting his Alban villa, these hours of
solitude were passed in wandering through the
columned arcades, where, on the walls, constructed
of a peculiar marble capable of bearing the highest
polish, he could perceive as he walked the shadow
of any one approaching from behind. Haunted
throughout his life by a constant terror of assas-
sination, his cowardly fears drove him to acts of
horrid cruelty. One courtier was murdered because he was born under a star promising imperial
power; another, because he carried about with
him a map of the world; another, because he had
invented a lance of a new shape. Cunning and
dissembling as he was cruel and remorseless,
Domitian began by caressing those whom he intended to destroy; but his honeyed phrases soon

became sentences of death, and those who sat beside him at the same couch, and eat of the same dish, were often, after a courteous reception, ordered out to instant execution. Naturally of a robust constitution, his monstrous excesses so wasted his strength that his hair fell from his head, his legs shrunk, his body swelled, and he became so incapable of all fatigue that he was generally carried about in a litter. The only manly exercise in which he delighted was archery. It is related that when passing the summer months in these delightful solitudes, the quantity of wild beasts he shot was quite incredible. So skilful was he in the use of the bow, that taking a little slave for his mark, he would shoot arrows through every finger of his upraised hand without so much as grazing the skin.

Such was the emperor who inhabited the walls under which I have been standing. Surrounded by all the splendour, riches, luxuries, and amusements that the empire of the world could bestow, he lived a trembling, suspicious wretch, incapable of enjoying the present, and tormented by dreary presentiments of the future. A haunting gloom seems yet to linger around the dark trees whose branches wave over the scattered ruins; a curse, heavy and palpable, hangs about their shadows.

As I looked, the spirit of the Past uprose so grim and horrible, so soiled with unutterable deeds of darkness, that I turned with horror from the fatal spot.

Leaving the Rospigliosi gardens, I emerged close by the tomb of Pompey, on the *regina viarum*, the Appian Way, whose every stone seems alive with the history of the past. After the imperial Cæsars—those magnificent masters of the material world—perhaps no single names stand out in such strong relief as those of St. Paul and Horace, who each have left recorded in their writings the day and the hour (so to say) when they passed over its massive pavement eighteen centuries ago. The beautiful legend connecting St. Paul with the Appian Way I have already noticed.

In the year 713, Mecænas, Cocceius, and Capitonius were sent by the senate to Brundusium, in order to effect a reconciliation between Augustus and Antony, who was then besieging that city. Horace accompanied his friends, and in celebrating this expedition has left a most interesting description of the journey, showing how, for the first two stages, they pursued the Appian way. (See Satire V., Book I.)

I have already mentioned Albano, *à propos* of

the delightful though hurried excursion I made there. I had now more time to view it at leisure. The modern town, a long straggling street, occupies a portion of what was the imperial villa. It is, to my mind, a hot stuffy place, abounding with donkeys and vulgarity. One sees the same *blasé* faces, the same impertinent *flâneurs* that haunted one on the Corso at Rome. Coming from the religious silence of our mountain retreat, it appeared to me an insufferable scene of confusion, dust, and tawdriness.

I put up my horse at the *locanda*, and strolled into the grounds of the Villa Doria. An English garden, gay with flowers, slopes towards the south, while the surrounding grounds are belted with woods, where one enjoys the sea breezes wafted over the adjacent olive-gardens. A pile of ruins and subterraneous excavations in the thickest portion of the grove mark the supposed sight of Pompey's favourite country palace, whither the devoted Cornelia bore his ashes, after he was murdered by the treacherous Ptolemy. His ruined sepulchre outside the gates of Albano I have already described.

Pompey, in the few peaceful intervals of his chequered life, appears to have preferred the amusements of the country to the cares and anxieties of the ever unquiet Forum. Plutarch, indeed, reproaches him for leaving his friends and soldiers to rove about Italy from one villa to another with his first wife Julia, the daughter of Cæsar, to whom he was passionately attached. Although he was considerably her senior, and not at all attractive in person, she returned his love with the utmost affection; "but," says the shrewd old biographer, "it was the charm of his *fidelity*, together with his conversation, which, notwithstanding his natural gravity, was particularly agreeable." When Julia died, Pompey came to this villa, where they had so often resided together, to solemnise the ceremony of her interment; but the people, out of regard to him, seized on her corpse, and insisted on burying it in the Campus Martius. At Julia's death the alliance between himself and Cæsar ended, and that fatal war, destined so soon to end his brilliant career, broke out.

It is related in his life that Cicero, having offended Cæsar by the execution of Lentulus and Cethegus, two leaders of the Catiline conspiracy, was informed he would either be obliged to defend himself by the sword or to go into exile. In this dilemma he resolved to apply to Pompey (hitherto his friend) to act as a mediator. But Pompey, then the husband of Cæsar's daughter, purposely absented himself at his Alban villa; and when informed by Piso, Cicero's son-in-law, that the great orator waited without to speak to him, he, not being able to bear the sight of his former friend in such miserable circumstances (his friend who had fought such worthy battles for him, and rendered him so many important services in the course of his administration), actually escaped out of the house by a back-door. As I looked at the scattered ruins which once formed the villa, the whole scene rose vividly before me, and the idea of great Pompey escaping by a back-door particularly diverted me.

Now I must tell you more of the vagaries of our Rocca life. We have had a grand festa—yes, indeed, a festa which has turned us all *sotto sopra* —in honour of the *Madonna del Tufo*. The origin of this festa is worth relating. At the top of the town a beautiful terrace-walk overshadowed by venerable trees skirts the face of the richly-wooded heights—a walk poised, as it were, in mid-air, 'twixt earth and heaven. At the end of this walk—the Corso of the Rocca—is a small church under an overhanging cliff. A stranger would stare at seeing that the altar is constructed of a great shapeless mass of tufa-rock (which the

people reverently kiss), and that little frescoes on
the walls record the fall of this rock. Now the
story goes that three travellers once passed along
this road in winter. The thunder rolled through
the woods; the lightning glared fiercely athwart the
Campagna; all Nature was convulsed. Suddenly
a portion of the rocky bank, wrenched violently
from its foundation, came thundering down the
cliff towards the narrow terrace-road. The travellers heard the crash, and gave up all hope of
life. Below was a precipice, above a mountain;
no escape seemed possible. They called wildly
on the Madonna—they lifted their hands in prayer
—when, wonderful to relate, at the very moment
that the rocky mass was suspended over their
heads, the Madonna, bearing her Jesus-child, appeared. Ay, appeared on the very rock which in
an instant more would engulf them; and lo! the
huge mass was miraculously turned aside, and
crashed down the fearful chasm below, leaving
the travellers unhurt. In gratitude they vowed a
shrine here to the Virgin Mother, where she is
invoked by the name of "Our Lady of the Rock."
The rock, raised by incredible labour, now forms
the altar, and is looked on, as Maria says, *come
una cosa di grandissima devozione.*" It is a pretty,
simple church, nestling under the crags on a little

platform overlooking the Lake of Albano, whose waters sleep calmly below.

The inhabitants all vie with each other at the Rocca who shall most honour the Virgin—their *own* Madonna, as they fondly call her. It is a festa known far and wide; crowds come from Rome and the environs to kneel at the shrine, and spend a joyous day in the breezy woods. When the morning came, you would have thought our little place was gone clean mad. Cannons were fired from the ruined fortress; scores of carriages laden with gentry and holiday folks lined the roads; horsemen and donkeymen came up by hundreds; the street was all astir—such a hum of voices, such ringing laughter, such smiles and sparkling eyes on every side! Men and maidens donned their best; crimson and yellow draperies floated from the houses; the bells rang cheerily out; the band from Frascati played martial airs; garlands of evergreens festooned the walls; and torches stood ready in the streets, wreathed with flowers, to be lighted in the evening. Then came the procession winding down from the Duomo, and very pretty it looked against the dark walls of the quaint old houses. There were priests walking two and two, habited in white and red, and followed by small acolytes swinging censers;

then came a great banner on poles painted in
radiant colours; then more priests, and a huge
cross made of rough wood, painfully recalling
"the accursed tree;" then another great banner,
which, as there was a fresh wind blowing, was
very nearly ascending bodily into the ambient air,
the poor standard-bearers making the drollest
grimaces as they frantically called on their fellows to assist them. Then came more crosses
and some big lanterns. The low chanting of the
choir rose in solemn cadence, one group taking
up the anthem, then another—a grave and melancholy music exceedingly impressive. Then
clouds of incense rose in streams of rich perfume,
"the sad and warning strains" falling more
earnestly upon the ear; then the priests prayed
with greater unction; at last, descending the hill,
appeared a famous miraculous picture in a heavy,
lumbering frame, raised on a kind of stand, and
borne on the shoulders of a dozen men. Like
most miraculous paintings, it was as dark and
black as night to eyes profane. In front walked
the high-priest (*achidiacono*), a grand-looking personage in flowing robes, diligently reciting prayers.
And then came a perfect sea of contadine, pressing, crowding about the venerated image with
eager enthusiasm; their snowy head-gear, scarlet

bodices, golden crosses, ear-rings, and floating draperies of lace and ribbon lending life and animation to the scene. All fell prostrate on their knees as the picture passed—the pretty ladies in the balcony opposite, the ragged urchins in the streets, the handsome baker, and our fat *nouveau riche* landlord, who, with all his vices, professes to be a devoted knight of the Madonna. It was very impressive to watch that simple yet earnest crowd, so hushed and silent; and to listen to the echoing chants, like soft voices of guardian angels, ever and anon bursting forth in a pæan of love and praise; while in front stretched the wide Campagna, trackless, boundless, like a golden sea, melting into mystic fields of loveliest blue and richest purple. After the miraculous picture came files of monks, white-robed Trinitarians, the red and blue cross embroidered on their breasts; and brown-habited Franciscans (*Osservanti*), with shaven crowns and hempen girdles; and two old priests leading pretty children dressed as angels, graceful smooth-faced things, their long, tangling hair garlanded with flowers hanging down over blue and white draperies, their small sandalled feet daintily pressing the rude stones. Such *concetti* as these might not be expedient elsewhere, but here in the sunny South, the land of ideality and symbolism, they are both appropriate and suggestive.

After the procession had passed we sallied out to see the humours of this religious fair. Along the terrace-walk the fun waxed fast and furious. Such thousands of people, such dust, such a braying of donkeys, and such a sun!—it was altogether overwhelming. Hundreds of stalwart young Roman peasants were there, their jackets thrown jauntily over one shoulder; and hosts of lovely girls in every variety of picturesque costume, rural Venuses these, village Circes, with wicked eyes and bright olive complexions, determined to slay no end of hearts. 'Twas *such* a picture, with the various groups passing and repassing against the browned masses of old rock, all carpeted with graceful plants, or emerging from under the broad sweeping branches of the large chestnut trees, whose silvery trunks gleamed in the chequered shade! The noise, the laughter, the mad rushing to and fro of ponies and donkeys, regardless where they went, or whom they upset, the vendors of fruit, and pictures, and cakes, all screaming in inharmonious unison, were prodigious.

"*Signora, tanta buona—un bajocco la libbra, frutta fresca freschissima—Ecco signora, guardi, la Madonna, la Madonna del Tufo, il sommo miracolo,* for a halfpenny—Buy the *Madonna, tanta buona,* for one halfpenny!—*Fiori*—a bouquet—*sua Signoria* must have a flower for the *buona festa—Fiori! Ecco! Fiori! Hi!—Ha!—Venite tutti quanti!*"

The nearer we approached the church the more the Babel increased. The crowd making its way in and out was tremendous. Such kneelings, such kissings, such frantic mutterings of prayers around the altar, now begemmed and bespangled with gold and tinsel! Those who one instant were vociferating, and swearing, and gesticulating, as if possessed by seven devils, the next moment were prostrate on the earth, repeating *Aves* as fast as they could gabble. Girls, who a second before had been looking *such* things out of their lustrous eyes, were now devoutly repeating their coronas, as if such mischievous animals as men were not in existence. Naughty roaring babies, rampaging boys, were schooled into silence. The very dogs which forced themselves in with their masters behaved with orthodox propriety.

Stuck up outside the church was a daub representing an old woman sitting by a table piled with gold, while from beneath the table a monster, neither flesh, fowl, nor fish, glared at her with

unearthly eyes—a most hideous beast. An old
blind man supported the picture, while his wife,
gifted with extraordinary loquacity, repeated the
story—"*Di una vecchia vedovella, miserabile il suo
stato, nella città di Milano.*"

An immense crowd speedily assembled.

"*Signori Cristiani, per l'amore della Madonna*,
give me a penny!" cried the blind man in a hollow voice, which served as a kind of under-cur-
rent, in the style of a Greek chorus, to the shouts
of his wife, who repeated the wonderful adventures
of Caterina and the *Fantasmo.*

"*Ascoltate—excellenze* all and every one—listen
while I relate the miserable story of the *vedovella*
of Milano. One night, in a vision, she heard a
voice—surely it was the voice of the *diavolo* himself—and the voice said: 'Go, Caterina, to the
loteria, and choose the number 5; thou shalt win
—*ve lo prometto.*' When morning was come,
Caterina went, but the gold—she had no gold to
buy his lottery ticket." . . . .

Here the woman paused.

"*Cristiani*, great noble, excellent signors, for
the love of our *own* Madonna, give me a *bajocco!*"
groaned out her husband.

A few pieces clinked in his bag.

"A neighbour, *sua amica*—a loving and kind

18*

neighbour, *tanta Cristiana*, had no gold, but lent Caterina a counterpane when she asked for it, which the wicked Caterina (ah! *peccatrice!*) went and pawned. Yes, pawned the counterpane her friend had lent her, because she said she was cold and *povera, povera. Ahi! la povertà! Miseri noi.* Then with the money she bought the number, and gained the prize—*si, amici miei*, Caterina gained a great prize. But her friend, *quella Cristiana che non era Cristiana*—having discovered by chance what had happened, possessed by the *demonio* (all the saints guard us from the temptation of the devil!), full of envy and rage, whispered it into the ear of her *cavaliere—un certo carabiniere*—who spoke and said: 'Maria, I know how that money is to be got.' Then that sinner, the *carabiniere*, took pitch, and paint, and hair, and blood, and bones, and in an instant made himself into a horrible *Fantasmo*, and at midnight, when the pale dead walk forth from their graves in winding-sheets, this *scellerato*——"

The blind man, who had long been threatening an interruption, was no longer to be appeased.

"*Excellenze*, by the pains of purgatory, a *bajocco!* I will pray for you all, *buoni Cristiani*, seven *Aves*, and four *Glorias. Cristiani, signori,* listen—I will pray—may your souls rest in peace a *bajocco*—a single one. Excellent good country-men, for the sake of my wife's fine *racconto*, money, *per pietà!*"

"*Zigarri, zigarri,* good *zigarri!*" broke in from the other side a limping beggar, thinking the moment opportune to sell his wares while the crowd was collected. But this new actor on the scene was summarily ejected by the united efforts of the crowd, now deeply interested in the *orrido Fantasmo* and the blind man's wife, who fought like a cur who finds another of his species prowling on his peculiar walk.

"Thanking the excellent company for the charity shown to the poor *cieco* my husband, and with the *permesso* of the *società,* I shall recommence. This wicked *scellerato* the *carabiniere* hid himself in Caterina's room, and in the silence of the night, after making certain fearful *rumori* such as the devils do in the Inferno, he spoke in these words:—

"'Caterina, Caterina, in the power of the Evil One art thou; give me the money, or I carry thee in my claws swift off to hell.'"

"*Ah! Cristiani, pensa ai dolori del inferno!* help us, good friends—money—a *bajocco!*" cried the *cieco.*

But at this interesting moment, when all stood transfixed in horrified curiosity (especially one pretty girl sitting at a table hard by, drinking wine, who by turns flirted with a crowd of *cavalieri*, then, growing pale at all these images of the devil and purgatory, crossed herself devoutly), the arrival of a large party of American friends from Albano deprived us of the conclusion of this lamentable tragedy.

By this time numerous parties had bivouacked in the woods, and were preparing to dine under the shade of the chestnut trees. The orthodox dish on this day was roast pig, that unclean animal being in some incomprehensible manner connected with the festa of the Madonna. Roast pig was selling piping hot in all directions, and very good it looked; but as we had a famous *chef* at home, we preferred domestic luxuries, with plates and spoons, to an Arcadian meal on the ground.

In the evening fireworks were let off just under our house, and exceedingly brilliant they were— fountains of fire, lakes of sulphur emitting blue sparks, rockets for a moment mocking the mildly-twinkling stars, then Icarus-like falling back in glittering showers. We had a temple of silver, mountains of gold, and all sorts of gaudy marvels,

concluding with a grand *girandola* that shot forth
a world of light, popping and fizzing like an
angry monster. Then calm, unsullied night
closed over the moving scene; and the moon
rode high, casting gigantic shadows over the vague
space below. So ended the great festa day at
Rocca di Papa.

Our great man here is the baker, who stands
all day smoking within the *portone* of his house,
his red cap hitched on one side of his head. A
jolly dog is the baker, Teresina's lover, as all the
world knows, for the *società* go to his house every
evening to a kind of club, and drink wine and
play cards until far into the night, making the
little street echo to their carouse. What roars of
laughter, what riotous, joyous choruses have often
"murdered sleep" from over the way! Sometimes
they have an *accademia* and really delightful
music. A flute is particularly "brave" on these
occasions, and sends forth the most aërial music,
wafted to us by the night breezes. Then there is
a guitar twanging joyous *ritornelli*, recalling bright
Venice, with its dark, gliding gondolas, its love
and its poetry. At other times a solitary song is
heard. Now, could you believe that these melodious whispers, floating "through regions mild
and calm," are all emanations from the baker's;

and that when the delicious music has sighed away, there is a rude riotous chorus, and shouts of *Bis* and *Bravo*, bringing one's poetic enthusiasm down suddenly to zero? Such are the vivid contrasts of our mountain home—idyllic poetry and *bourgeois* prose.

A principal character at the baker's is the Sicilian *cavaliere*, a dot of a man, made up altogether of a stentorian voice—a very Goliath to speak withal, who talks as fast as Figaro in a passion, and thumps the table as he gives you the latest news from Rome in a quite Neapolitan shower of words. Count Dionigi, who lodges below, abominates the baker and his jovial club, and looks indignant if you admire the music. Dionigi, called by the Italians *Fosseficato*, or the Fossil, lives at Città Lavinia, the ancient Lanuvium, and has never, during the last fifty years, been known to change one iota—neither growing older nor younger, fatter nor thinner, but remaining ever the same starched little figure, with the same well-regulated grey hair. If all the world were turned into dust, not a grain would rest on his immaculate blue coat—dust and that coat are as antagonistic as the poles. Dionigi has never married. A wife would be *de trop* to such a male old maid; and as for children—pah! When he comes to see me he makes a *riverenza* like a dancing-master, rises on his toes, and gracefully advancing, repeats that I am "an angel, a divinity," with a stiff little bow at the close of each well-used phrase. Then down he sits, hat in hand, crossing his tiny knees—the funny little manikin! His exits are capital; he rises, bows, and says "he will raise the *incomodo;*" shoulders his stick, which always plays a principal part in his little drama; stands erect; bows; retreats; then bows again, repeating at each move, "*I miei rispetti— Signora bella, amabile*"—spreading his polite blessings from side to side like a priest at mass. They say Dionigi has something to do with a very romantic story, of which I am anxious to learn the particulars.

Among our characters, Giuseppe della Fante, our *maestro di casa*, must not be forgotten; he who, according to his own account, is sprung from a decayed Roman family, has once been a soldier, and cannot accommodate himself pleasantly to his altered fortunes. There he stands at the baker's door, cigar in mouth, with his great moustache, military cap, full French trousers, big enough to make an ordinary woman's petticoat, and his spurs—those eternal spurs! Seeing that he never rides more than once a week, and then on the back of a wretched pony, those spurs are a mystery to us. "*Ma*," as the Italians say, "*fanno impressione*." Certainly there is some sympathetic affinity between the extinct glories of the Delle Fante line and those spurs in Giuseppe's mind. How he chaffs with the pretty maidens skipping in to buy bread! How he gossips with the doctor and the *priore!* How he patronises the *carabinieri*, and kicks the dirty urchins who presume to touch those sacred spurs! All this and much more you should see with your own eyes. He is a regular Italian, violent, excitable, impressionable, easily offended, yet so devoted, generous, and self-forgetting, that one really ends by admiring his very faults. Speak kindly to him, and tears spring up like dewdrops in his sparkling, brigand-looking eyes; ask him to do any wonderful thing—to ride to Rome in an hour, to scale a precipice for the sake of a flower, to hunt the woods for a favourite bird—and he rushes forth with as chivalrous a good-will as the veriest carpet-knight that ever donned a lady's scarf.

The quarrels he gets into, the imaginary battles he fights, the bloody recitals with which he regales the select audience at the baker's—recitals about stilettoes and pistols, encounters with banditti, gaping wounds, threats of vengeance and

extermination against his enemies generally—
bagatelle! come vi pare!   Then the adventures he
has encountered (Heaven only knows whether they
be romance or truth)—the grandeur of his appearance on festa days, his tender care of my
children, with whom, if they are merry, he romps
after the fashion of an old dog lying down to be
kicked—his savage ill-humour if his dignity be
offended—his bursts of passion—his humble
apologies—his alternate smiles and frowns, make
up quite an epitome of human life.   Poor Giuseppe,
genuine child of the South, thou hast the vices
and virtues of thy race and of thy clime, but thou
hast an honest and a kindly heart!

CHAPTER X.

Feast of SS. Peter and Paul—St. Peter's Illuminated—
The Girandola.

THE Feast of SS. Peter and Paul is the birth-
day of Rome. Heat and the fear of malaria
have by that time driven every foreigner away—
which was to me an especial recommendation.
So, in the early morning, before the mid-day sun
had become dangerously hot, I traversed the
parched Campagna, and found myself at the
Lateran Gate.

Everything told of heat and a raging Italian
sun. People sat pale and exhausted at the shop-
doors, armed with paper whisks with which
languidly to drive away the flies; little extempore
fountains bubbled up on tiny tables spread with
delicious pulpy lemons, and *acque dolci* (sweet
drinks) cooled with fresh vine-leaves. Every
woman and child we passed, of whatever degree,
carried a fan, which she used industriously;
the very beggars shook their tin boxes in one

hand, and fanned themselves with the other. All labours, trades, and occupations were carried on in the streets, which, never too wide, were now almost choked up. Shoemakers were making shoes; tailors were sitting cross-legged on tables squeezed up against their house-walls; women were cutting and stitching on low stools, surrounded by their gipsy-eyed progeny; girls were combing each other's hair (often a severe test of friendship in hot weather); and men were walking under the eaves with their hats in their hands, all pale, worn, exhausted. The three-legged tables outside the cafés were crowded with sleepy or sleeping men: the scarcely-awake were indulging in ices or drinks—the sleepers were lying about in the strangest attitudes; for an Italian could sleep, I believe, on one leg, if he tried. It being about noon, the street kitchens were in active operation—fish, flesh, and fowl hissing and broiling over pans of charcoal; and stands of fruit, apricots, figs, and cherries, ripe and ready to drop into one's mouth.

When we reached the English quarter, the Piazza di Spagna, great were the emptiness and the desolation. The windows in the hotels were hermetically sealed, and the doors shut. Piale's library was a wilderness. Not a soul was to be seen. The long flight of the Trinità steps was scorching and vacant. The little fountains at its base bubbled in an utter solitude. No groups of peasants were lounging there *en tableaux*. The man who does the venerable father with long beard and patriarchal garments—a special rascal; and the young man with the high-art features, who does the saints and apostles with a glory round his head; the beauty-peasant with yards of white drapery folded over her glossy braids, under which glow the impudent glancing eyes, coral beads, and gold necklace—all gone, driven out by the heat! Gone, too, was that dear little boy who sat for an angel when he was not stretching out his little dimpled hand, asking, like Oliver, for "more," and his father, clad in sheep-skins, who, with slouched hat and ragged cloak, did the everlasting conspirator.

Such is Rome in the dog-days—no life, no carriages, no sound; like the enchanted city in the Arabian Nights, all lay sunk in slumber. We descended, as the polite French say, at the Palazzo M——, where apartments had been secured—a noble residence, big enough to take up one side of a square, with *salons* so large that people looked dim and misty at the further end. That very evening St. Peter's was to be illuminated;

so, after fortifying ourselves with an excellent
dinner, sent in piping hot in a tin box from a
neighbouring *trattoria*, and further recruiting ourselves by draughts of refreshing Orvieto out of
wicker bottles, we attained that contented and
happy state of mind proper to the eve of a great
festa.   Evening, delicious, balmy evening, had
come; the breeze swept through the streets, and
the stars peeped out as we started—together with
hundreds and thousands of the Pope's undutiful
subjects—for St. Peter's.   On these grand occasions the Ponte Sant' Angelo is closed to the
vulgar, who are obliged to pass over the Tiber
into the Trastevere.   Plunging into the narrow
streets that lead thither, the site of the home of
Raphael's Fornarina was pointed out to me.   It
is now a small two-windowed house, the lower
portion used as a magazine of herbs—Anglicè,
the greengrocery business.   While our carriage is
slowly advancing through labyrinths of streets,
every now and then stopped by the *carabinieri*
(here acting as policemen), who rush upon us with
drawn swords, I will tell my readers the real story
of Raphael and the Fornarina.

When Raphael was painting his beautiful
frescoes in the Farnesina Palace in the Trastevere,
he passed daily over the bridge and through this

narrow street to his work. One day, it is said, he saw a beautiful black-haired girl, of the voluptuous type painters love so well, bathing her white feet in the waters of the Tiber. From that hour all peace of mind forsook him, and he forgot even art in his earnest desire to be loved by her. The baker's daughter, however, was already provided with a lover, a certain fierce soldier stained with the blood of many battles, who aspired to the possession of this peerless beauty. Egidio had no refinement of soul, no "intellect of love;" but the outward charms of the girl had touched him, and he swore that if any one else presumed to approach her, he would finish him with a *stoccata*. Catterinella, never having known the delicious frenzy of love, had hitherto submitted with that grace which arises from perfect indifference to the advances of the soldier. He often came to her father's shop, and gossiped and smoked, until she grew used to him, and Egidio, in a manner became domesticated. But when Raphael came also, and talked, and cast loving glances out of his beautiful eyes at Catterinella, she began to detest the soldier, and to feel all the joys and pains of first love. Raphael not only rapidly insinuated himself into her heart, but with that amiability and grace which he so eminently possessed, fascinated even the rough baker himself. He was too much absorbed in his art to spend much time at the shop, but that very art afforded him the readiest means of advancing his suit. He asked Giuseppe to allow his daughter to sit to him for her picture; and he, though but a common vulgar tradesman, still had enough respect for the fine arts, then so generally cultivated in Rome, to consider the request as a compliment, and to comply. But he made Raphael promise never to mention his compliance, both out of regard to Catterinella's fair fame, and for fear of the rough soldier, Egidio, whose blind jealousy might prompt him to commit some violence. When Catterinella first went to Raphael's studio it was secretly and cautiously, and accompanied by her mother; but so frequent were the visits of Egidio, and so ardent his passion for Catterinella, that it was impossible for their absence not to raise his suspicions. One day when they had left the shop, as they supposed unobserved, he watched them, and, seeing them enter a doorway and ascend a staircase, followed. The door was inadvertently left open. Egidio entered, and stealing noiselessly into the spacious studio, hid himself among some lumber. Unable to control his fierce passions at seeing Catterinella seated opposite Raphael, Egidio drew his stiletto and rushed on the painter, who, at that very instant poising his brush in the air, was intently and passionately examining the Fornarina's features. The women, horrified at the sudden apparition of Egidio, his naked dagger and horrid looks, screamed aloud; but Raphael, unarmed as he was, rose and faced his assailant. No sooner did Egidio recognise Sanzio as the detested rival whom he was about to murder—Sanzio, whom he regarded as a deity, whom he had heard celebrated as the very wonder of the world—than he stood transfixed, and the stiletto dropped from his hand. A few inarticulate words of excuse and prayers for pardon fell from his lips. Touched by the humane looks of Raphael, who gazed on him with a kind of pitying astonishment, Egidio endeavoured, in broken words, to explain the motives which had induced this murderous attack. He spoke of his love; he pleaded his jealousy. Then he turned towards the affrighted Catterinella, who, scared by his fierce looks, scarcely dared to raise her head, while he himself, speaking with ill-suppressed passion, implored her to be calm. He assured her he would not injure her, but he conjured her, by all she held most sacred, to tell him if she really loved him. Catterinella, inspired by the passionate excitement of the moment, forgot her fears of Egidio, his cruelty, his jealousy; she forgot all save Raphael—the sun under whose rays she had expanded into a new and delicious life—Raphael, the god of her idolatry, who stood pale and speechless before her. Raising her eyes to his face, she acknowledged the love she had long secretly cherished in her heart, and confessed in faltering accents that he was dear to her beyond all other mortals. Egidio was struck dumb. Seizing his dagger, which had fallen on the floor, he rushed from the studio. Relieved from the fascination of Raphael's countenance and majestic presence, Egidio, grasping his weapon in his hand, resolved to return and murder him; but when he remembered the words of Catterinella—when he recalled those passionate words in which she had confessed her love—his resolution again changed. "Why kill him because she loves me no longer?" exclaimed he. Honour and despair strove in the breast of the savage soldier. Love, hope, life— all had passed into the possession of another, and that other a man so godlike that he could scarcely, even in the wild paroxysms of his rage, wonder at the preference. His violent nature could not endure such torture, and, in utter despair, he plunged into his own breast the weapon he had raised against Sanzio.

As we turned into the Lungara every palace was illuminated with red lights. The immense Corsini Palace shone out brilliantly, and looked the very image of a magnificent feudal residence. Lights glittered along its immense façade, row above row to the very roof, while at intervals along the street were planted huge torches of burning pitch that blazed and flashed and cast ruddy unearthly tints on the white palace behind, while great bonfires of tar-barrels, poked up by men with long poles, flared away on the ground. Immovable in the doorway stood the porter, *bâton* in hand—a mass of lace, badges, and cocked hat, evidently convinced that the whole dignity of the Corsini line consisted in his majestic deportment. A little crowding, some swearing, and a great amount of butting from the *carabinieri*, who ride full tilt at man, horse, or carriage that offends them, and we were within the colonnade of St. Peter's, that noble colonnade now glittering with lights, whose outstretched arms seemed to clasp in one embrace all the people of the universe. Never does St. Peter's look so beautiful as when illuminated. The magnificent building, with its encircling colonnades; its topmost cupola; its population of saints, prophets, angels, and apostles crowding the roof; and the cross surmounting all, hangs amid the very stars, a glittering vision. It is not in the power of words to convey any adequate notion of St. Peter's that night; each pillar, each arch in the mighty structure, was marked out by lines of mellowed light below, above, around, not massed in any one place, but gracefully following the lines and undulations of the vast fabric.

For awhile we contemplated what is called the *silver* illumination, when the lights are veiled. Exactly one hour and a quarter after the first hour of night a cannon was fired from the fort of Sant' Angelo. The harmonious bells of St. Peter's tolled out in response, and in a moment, in the twinkling of an eye, streams of ruddy light flashed up from below into the colonnades, marking their elegant outlines, through a thousand glittering columns. What had been pale subdued light now blazed forth in flakes of ruddy fire. The great basilica was enveloped in streams of quivering brightness, its gigantic front, white as alabaster, standing out with a strange clearness on a background of flames. Great vases of burning pitch, provided as if by enchantment, suddenly burst out between every column in the vast colonnade;

every statue burned with a living light, that rose up and flared, as the wind caught the forked flames, like a universal conflagration. The cupola especially, beautifully relieved by the dark sky behind, flashed out in a blaze of the most dazzling splendour; while above, surmounting all, the radiant cross shone with indescribable brilliancy —a brand as it were snatched from heaven. It was beautiful to see the gushing fountains reflecting thousands of lamps in their pure water; shooting up in liquid pillars to fall back a foamy mass of molten silver; cooling the air and sending out clouds of delicious spray. Then the bells broke forth in merry chimes, deep-toned and musical; military bands struck up in the piazza; and the cannon from Sant' Angelo boomed distinctly above all other sounds.

Next morning (St. Peter's Day) we rose very early, to attend high mass at St. Peter's Church, the ceremonies being precisely similar to those which take place at Easter, with this notable difference, that Romans, not English and Americans, form the congregation. Every one flocked to the all-embracing arms of that great piazza, and we soon fell into a long line of carriages slowly advancing towards the basilica. Again we crossed the muddy Tiber, its volume much lessened by the rainless summer. The houses and palaces bordering the river, always of a peculiarly mellow warm tint, now looked baked with the fierce heat. Clouds of fine small dust rose in the light summer breeze. Altogether, it was a great relief to be again engulfed in the narrow, shady streets of the Trastevere. Every passage and cranny leading to St. Peter's was choked and overflowing with an ever-increasing multitude. They came in boats; they came in grand equipages; in humble *baroccini;* on foot; to worship at that magnificent shrine.

Streams of people spread over the piazza, and, mounting the steps, were engulfed by the great portals. We entered. The mellow light of morning subdued the too glaring details of the florid architecture. The church was in grand gala, walls and pillars draped with red and gold, assimilating harmoniously with the brilliant coloured marbles and mosaics. The cupola, rising like a firmament, shone in the slanting rays of the morning sun— angels, saints, and prophets emblazoned in bright colours on the golden frescoes. Beneath, the altar was spread with the costliest vessels of gold, chalices, cups, salvers, and crosses carved by the hands of Cellini or Bramante, all radiant with sparkling jewels.

On either side were enclosures prepared for

the ladies, who came in black veils and dresses
de rigueur; but instead of the irreverent Easter
crowd rushing, pushing, laughing, and talking, as
if in the crush-room of the opera, the seats were
thinly occupied by a sprinkling of ladies, whose
devout looks showed that they came to pray, and
not to stare. The tribune behind the high-altar
was hung with crimson, and to the left stood a
throne prepared for the Pope. Down the central
aisle an avenue was formed by the civic guard and
the quaint Swiss soldiers, through which his holiness was to pass. We were scarcely settled when
a hush and a general motion of expectation announced that the Pope had arrived at the central
door. Slowly and silently the magnificent procession passed up towards the altar. First came the
Swiss guards, and the chamberlains in red silk.
Then Pius, seated on the "gestorial" chair or
throne, glittering with gold, purple, and crimson,
wearing his triple crown, and habited in robes of
white. Over him was borne a dais of crimson
and gold, while beside him were carried two great
fans of peacock's feathers, typical of immortality.
There is a look of Eastern magnificence about
these fans extremely striking. The Pope, calm and
majestic, dispensed blessings as he passed with
the air of one wrapped in deep devotion. He

was followed by the entire Sacred College, all
aglow with crimson and guipure lace, a sight calculated to break any lady's heart on the score of
misplaced finery. Chaplains, secretaries, and
chamberlains (mere minnows to these ecclesiastical Tritons) fluttered in their rear, followed by
files of the superbly-dressed Guardia Nobile, all
picked men, tall, graceful, handsome; disciplined
in the encounters of social warfare and "carpet
knighthood;" now superb in glistening helmets,
short scarlet mantles, and a generally classic air,
reminding one of Pollio in *Norma*, whose social
line of conduct, as well as outward costume, they
are said to emulate. The Pope was now seated
on his throne, and the mass began.

It is to my mind a fatal want in the otherwise
noble ceremonial of the Papal mass at St. Peter's
that the music is entirely vocal. Part-singing,
however perfect, is monotonous. The Pope's
famous choristers are always invisible, caged like
singing-birds, in a golden-latticed gallery. The
Gregorian chant, although admirable as mediæval
music, becomes wearisome after two hours' duration, and the mass is long to exhaustion. The
Pope stands, walks, and kneels, sometimes at his
throne, sometimes at the high-altar, sometimes
alone, and sometimes surrounded by the cardinals.

One wonders how he can remember such constant
changes, unless one happens to know there is an
officer attached to the Papal court whose sole
business it is to prompt him, and to keep him
and the cardinals "well posted up" in their daily
duties—what dresses to wear, what to "eat, drink,
and avoid." Sometimes there is a pause, the
music ceases, the Pope and cardinals sit enthroned
(Anglicè, rest themselves), and the golden vessels
are moved and removed on the high-altar. During
one of these pauses I looked round at the groups
near the high-altar (where the mere vulgar crowd
is not allowed to penetrate) and wondered at the
curiously mediæval aspect of the scene. Here
were party-coloured Swiss guards, red, yellow,
and black, with steel caps and corslets, commanded by officers in complete armour of polished
steel inlaid with gold, some actually wearing steel-
chain tunics over crimson velvet, with golden
helmets, so that when two or three whispered together they instantly formed a picture for Maclise
—Papal chamberlains, picturesque in high Elizabethan ruffs, doublets, gold chains, orders, long
hose, and rosetted shoes; regular Sir Walter
Raleighs, and, like him, remnants of a century
when Spain ruled European fashions as France
does now—priests breaking the mundane pageant

here and there, and reminding one of the mass
still proceeding (which, by reason of its length
and pauses, seemed over long before it really
was), in every kind, colour, and variety of gold-
embroidered vestments—officers in dark uniforms,
and officers in white uniforms, diligently keeping
back masses of Roman peasants, gaudy as butterflies as to body and petticoat, and quite laden
with chains and crosses, earrings and flowers,
gold, silver, and pearls; many of them wondrously
handsome women. To all these add rows of
black-veiled ladies. sitting on either side in the
reserved seats, backed by the many-coloured walls
rich with mosaics and variegated marbles up to
the very cupola, where, under a glare of light, the
four gigantic Evangelists in the spandrels of the
arches float in a haze of golden sunshine.

Again we settled down to the mass. The
Pope advanced to the altar, denuded of mitre and
royal trappings, and wearing a plain white dress.
The music ceased; the attendant prelates retired;
every knee was bent; every head bowed in seem-
ing devotion. Alone on the steps of the altar
stood that venerable old man, his hands clasped
over the elements, his eyes turned to heaven.
While he communicated, the silence was positively
awful. Then, stealing around, came the soft

sounds of the silver trumpets, low and plaintive,
at first, as wailing spirits, then swelling forth in a
hosanna of joy and praise. The Pope, holding
in his hand the host, turned to the four quarters
of the globe. The *Agnus Dei* was chanted; the
Pope resumed his robes and retired as he came,
bestowing blessings around; and the crowd, ebbing
and flowing like a human sea, cast its vast waves
through every open door into the piazza beyond,
where the burning sunshine caught and absorbed
them in its rays. We, too, with these thousands
of living victims, were ruthlessly clutched by that
burning monster, the sun, waiting to devour us
the instant we left the kindly shelter of the cool
sanctuary.

But the celebrations of Rome's great festa to
her patron saint were not yet over. Magnificent
pleasures were yet awaiting us in the Piazza del
Popolo at the first hour of night. The piazza is
now densely filled. The fountains and obelisks
rise out of acres of pleasure-loving Romans; galleries are erected in the porticoes of the twin
churches opposite the Flaminian Gate. Every window is filled, and every eye turned in expectant
eagerness towards the Pincian Hill, where amid
lofty terraces and sculptured trophies, gigantic
statues and dark ilex woods, the *girandola* (fire-

works) is to be exhibited.   Meanwhile, the usual
fanning and consuming of ices and of sweet drinks
goes on among the Roman princesses, seated on
a raised estrade, looking as haughty and unpleasant as any classical Cornelias or Volumnias
that history could furnish.

The herald cannon sound, and up fly millions
of rockets, descending in blue, red, purple, and
yellow stars.   When these brilliant comets allow
us to look round, the summit of the Pincian is
transformed into a great temple of fire, enclosed
by walls of quivering crystal, broken by niches
filled with fiery statues—a temple such as Vulcan
might have reared to Venus in the infernal shades.

Now volleys of deafening cannon rattle till
one's ears ache, and, behold! overlapping streams
of liquid fire rush down the steep sides of the
Pincian into the piazza, and mysteriously disappear in showers of golden sparks, which the
crowd struggles to catch; but, lo! they are gone!
Then we have an *intermezzo* of rockets and
catherine-wheels, the cannons all the time out-
doing one another; and now a burning palace
appears, with great halls and galleries, and endless arcades and colonnades, in fiery perspective,
red with palpitating flames.   Such a palace might
have suited the ghosts in Vathek, condemned to

wander hither and thither for ever through boundless vaults of fire, clasping a flaming heart under
folds of shadowy drapery.

I could not tell all the wonderful tricks and
changes of these marvellous fireworks. The en-
chanter Merlin never terrified his enemies with
more surprising displays of his transforming art.
As a final triumph, the whole Pincian became the
crater of a horrible volcano, belching forth fire
and flames, while the roar of cannon mimicked
the thunders of the labouring mountain. Red
lava-streams rushed down in every direction and
millions of rockets shot up into the heavens, to
fall back bright and glittering, like planets fallen
from their spheres.

A moment more, and all was over. The moon
shone down serenely in a soft twilight, casting
pale lights on the statues and terraced galleries,
as if all else had been a disordered dream.

And here my Diary ends. I am suddenly
called back to England, and "the Idle Woman"
(not so very idle after all) lays down her pen and
becomes "the woman of the period," with *really*
nothing to do!

THE END.

www.ingramcontent.com/pod-product-compliance
Lightning Source LLC
Chambersburg PA
CBHW020506270326
41926CB00008B/761